THE VIRGIN BIRTH
IN THE THEOLOGY OF THE ANCIENT CHURCH

STUDIES IN HISTORICAL THEOLOGY · 2

THE VIRGIN BIRTH IN THE THEOLOGY OF THE ANCIENT CHURCH

HANS VON CAMPENHAUSEN

Professor of Theology
in the University of Heidelberg

SCM PRESS LTD

BLOOMSBURY STREET LONDON

Translated by Frank Clarke from the German
Die Jungfrauengeburt in der Theologie der alten Kirche
(Sitzungsberichte der Heidelberger Akademie der Wissenschaften,
Philosophisch-historische Klasse, Jahrgang 1962, 3. Abhandlung)
Carl Winter Universitätsverlag, Heidelberg, 1962

CONTENTS

ABBREVIATIONS

BSFEM	*Bulletin de la Société Française d'Etudes Mariales*
BZNW	*Beihefte zur Zeitschrift für die neutestamentliche Wissenschaft*
CSCO	Corpus Scriptorum Christianorum Orientalium
CSEL	Corpus Scriptorum Ecclesiasticorum Latinorum
ET	English translation
GCS	Die Griechischen Christlichen Schriftsteller der ersten Jahrhunderte
HTR	*Harvard Theological Review*
JTS	*Journal of Theological Studies*
LMK	*Lexikon der Marienkunde*, Regensburg, 1957ff.
LTK	Buchberger, *Lexikon für Theologie und Kirche*, 2nd edition, Freiburg, 1957ff.
OCA	Orientalia Christiana Analecta (Rome)
PG	Migne, *Patrologia Graeca*
PL	Migne, *Patrologia Latina*
PO	R. Graffin and R. Nau, *Patrologia Orientalis*
RAC	*Reallexikon für Antike und Christentum*, Stuttgart, 1950ff.
RGG	*Die Religion in Geschichte und Gegenwart*, 3rd edition, Tübingen, 1957ff.
SC	Sources Chrétiennes
TLZ	*Theologische Literaturzeitung*
TQ	*Theologische Quartalschrift*
TU	Texte und Untersuchungen zur Geschichte der altchristlichen Literatur
TWNT	*Theologisches Wörterbuch zum Neuen Testament*, Stuttgart, 1932ff.
ZNW	*Zeitschrift für die neutestamentliche Wissenschaft*
ZRGG	*Zeitschrift für Religions- und Geistesgeschichte*
ZTK	*Zeitschrift für Theologie und Kirche*

The numbers at the head of each page indicate the pages of the German edition.

Introduction

IT NOT infrequently happens that the difficulty of treating a problem of scholarship is less in the lack than in the excess of attention that has been given to it; and this occurs nowhere more often than in the sphere of historical theology. The passionate interest which the subject-matter arouses in its students pushes research further and further; but it also tempts one continually to ask questions that cannot be answered, and to give answers that are really doubtful or unwarrantable. Thus there comes into being an immense body of specialized literature, which has failed to acquire knowledge in any proportion to the industry expended, and which by its suggestions, assertions, and refutations gives rise to further publications, and at last discourages anyone who does not wish to become a specialist in that particular field. Thus what is essential is smothered by what is incidental, what is permanently right by what is temporarily new, and ascertainable or long-established truth by the product of wishful thinking. Perspective and detachment, which are necessary preconditions for serious discussion, are lost, and the thicket threatens to become impenetrable.

The aim of the present work is to open up a path through this scholastic wilderness, the so-called 'Mariology' of the early Church. It cannot be seriously disputed that the early Church, at any rate during its first few centuries, knew no real Marian doctrine,[1] that is, no thematic theological concern with Mary's person and her significance in the scheme of salvation. Nevertheless the flood of publications relating to the subject is now beyond computation, and under the pressure of present Catholic dogmatic interest it is still rising. I should not have been able to write the following piece of

[1] Thus G. Söll, 'Die Mariologie der Kappadokier', *TQ* 131 (1951), 168, rightly emphasizes that 'before the Council of Ephesus none of the fathers offers a self-contained Mariology'.

research but for the many specialized works that have appeared in the last two decades; but I do not on that account claim to have been able completely to master even the literature that merits serious consideration; the mass of what is scientifically unsound and worthless, even though it is listed in numerous bibliographies,[1] is much too great for that. On the other hand, however, it does not seem to me desirable that the work of summarizing and orientating should be left exclusively to people who specialize within the narrowest limits. As far as I can see, we lack today a critical presentation of the development in the early Church, setting out historically the accumulated material in right proportion, and not mixing with it any points of view that modernize it. This was attempted two

[1] The titles relating to the subject are estimated at about 100,000 in 1959. A Marian Bibliography for works published since 1950 is now produced at intervals by G. Besutti as a supplement to *Marianum*. We cannot be surprised at the uninterrupted productivity in this sphere, if we merely try to realize the number of more or less scholarly so-called 'Marian Academies' and institutions. I am particularly grateful to Dr Kurt-Victor Selge for lightening the burden of such a laborious business.

Apart from the older eighteenth-century foundations—the 'Mitirtea' in Rome, the Warsaw Academy, and the Franciscan Marian Academy in Portugal— we may mention here the Papal Academy of the Immaculate Conception in Rome, the Bibliographic Marian Academy of Lerida, the Marian Academy at the Papal Athenaeum Salesianum in Turin, the Papal Theological Faculty 'Marianum' of the Servites (with the right to graduate and several Marian professorships), and (also granting diplomas) the Institutum Mariologiae and the Papal International Marian Academy in Rome, which itself publishes six series of writings on Mariology (already comprising about 100 volumes). There is also a Stabile Consilium Mariologico-Marianis Internationalibus Conventibus Provehendis, one of whose objects is to support the numerous national Marian societies and to establish new ones. International Marian Congresses (with Proceedings and so on) are now to be held every four years.

Of the Mariological periodicals, listed in part by René Laurentin, *Kurzer Traktat der mariologischen Theologie* (1959), perhaps the following may claim a scholarly character: *Mariale Dagen* (Tongerloo, since 1931); *Marianum* (Rome, since 1938); *Estudios Marianos* (Madrid, since 1942); *Estudios Marianos* (since 1944, 1 volume); *Marian Studies* (Washington, since 1950); *Ephemerides Mariologicae* (Madrid, since 1951); *Journées sacerdotales Mariales* (since 1952); *La nouvelle revue Mariale* (Montfort, since 1954, since 1957 under the title *Cahiers Marials*). There are also *Cahiers de Joséphologie* (Montreal, since 1953), in which, for example, the question is discussed how old Joseph was when he married Mary: J. J. Davis, 'The Age of St Joseph at the Time of his Marriage', *Cah. de Joséph.* 6 (1958), 225–66. After Mariology and Josephology we may perhaps in time *per analogiam* expect an 'Annalogy'.

generations ago by Lehner,[1] Lucius,[2] and Neubert,[3] whose works are no longer up to date. The present survey starts from the conviction that its subject-matter is not specially complicated or difficult, once we have resolved to keep to the fore the simple and obvious questions that present themselves, to disregard unnecessary reflections and speculations, and to arrange the material as far as possible in accordance with its various aspects.

In all this I shall intentionally keep within bounds. My concern in the following account is only with the statements made and the views represented about Mary within the theology of the early Church, and even with these only in so far as they are connected with the theme of the virgin birth of Christ;[4] for that is the starting-point, and it also remains in the first place the most essential content of we may call the Marian doctrine of the early Church. The history of popular devotion to Mary, the influence of which on theology is often overestimated, is outside our scope, nor shall I go into historical questions about the origin of religious motives and ideas. I shall follow the development as far as the beginning of the fifth century. That point sets a certain period to theological interpretation, and at the same time the Church's official Marian cult begins to develop, which from now on exercises a growing and clearly perceptible influence on the responsible speech and thought of theologians.

[1] F. A. Lehner, *Die Marienverehrung in den ersten zehn Jahrhunderten der Kirche* (1886²).

[2] Ernst Lucius, *Die Anfänge des Heiligenkults in der christlichen Kirche* (1904), Book 4: 'Maria', 420–504.

[3] E. Neubert, *Marie dans le dogme de l'Église anténicéenne* (Diss. Fribourg, 1908).

[4] The fruitfulness of such research has been rightly stressed by, e.g., Gustav Wingren, *Man and the Incarnation—a study in the Biblical Theology of Irenaeus* (1959), 97, n. 53.

I

The Establishment of the Tradition

BEFORE CONSIDERING the development of the theological dogma
we will say a little about the rise of the virgin birth tradition. Even
though, as has been said, we do not wish to pursue the problems
of comparative religion and form-criticism, it must be constantly
remembered that the legend of Jesus' virgin birth is anything but
the starting-point of the early Christian message. Indeed, it appears
in the New Testament in only two places, namely in the infancy
stories of Matthew's and Luke's Gospels; and in the course of
development it is at first taken up only on isolated occasions, and
not maintained without contradiction. That is a matter of fact, the
full implications of which do not generally become clear when one's
research is confined to primitive Christian tradition. It is, however,
an essential fact if we want to see the Christological development in
right perspective, and it is also of some importance for the initial
evaluation of and emphasis on the birth tradition.

If we are to follow the beginnings and the slow spread of the
virgin birth story, it is not enough to stop at the Gospel texts cited,
and to accept them, just as they stand, as the oldest tradition. On
the contrary, it appears on closer inspection that Matthew is already
taking opposite opinions into account, and that the Lucan infancy
legends themselves depend partly on material in an older form
which, as yet, knows nothing of the virgin birth. In this connection
I would refer to the textual analysis, unsurpassed as a whole, made
by Martin Dibelius in the Proceedings of the Heidelberg Academy;[1]
and in drawing on it I confine myself to essentials, leaving aside

---

[1] M. Dibelius, *Jungfrauensohn und Krippenkind. Untersuchungen zur Geburtsgeschichte Jesu im Lukas-Evangelium* (Sitzungsberichte der Heidelberger Akademie, phil.-hist. Klasse, 1932), reprinted in *Botschaft und Geschichte, Gesammelte
Aufsätze* I (1953), 1–78, from which it is cited; also a summary of the conclusions
in *From Tradition to Gospel* (ET, 1934), 123ff.

lesser disputable questions.[1] Luke's artistic introductory narrative is woven into a whole from various fragments of written or oral tradition, which are in part only slightly revised, and whose original character and import can still be clearly recognized in several passages, so that they can be appraised as coming independently from original sources. Accordingly the idea of a virgin birth seems to be in some degree firmly anchored only to the annunciation *pericope*.[2] Within the actual Nativity story Joseph and Mary are no doubt thought of as Jesus' actual parents.[3] In contrast to this, it may be that Matthew in the opening chapters of his Gospel already represents a somewhat later stage.[4] He everywhere takes the virgin birth for granted; but he already has to defend it against doubt and criticism—an intention far removed from Luke's naïve miracle-story. On the other hand, both the Lucan and the Matthean genealogical trees show that they originated in communities that as yet knew nothing of a virgin birth and regarded Jesus as Joseph's child,[5] for, although they differ from each other, they both relate only to Joseph.[6] Only in the last link in the chain have the evangelists attempted an artificial twist by way of correction, so as to accommodate it to the virgin birth; but the numerous variations of the tradition show how little its text satisfied its readers, even in very early times. The subsequent explanation that the genealogical trees should be taken as establishing and guaranteeing only the 'legal' and not the physical parentage of Jesus does not help; it is simply a makeshift for which there is no adequate basis.[7] As the genealogical trees

[1] As larger and valuable specialized works we may mention G. Erdmann, *Die Vorgeschichte des Lukas- und Matthäus-Evangeliums und Vergils vierte Ekloge* (1932), and René Laurentin, *Structure et Théologie de Luc I–II* (1957).
[2] Luke 1.26–38, though this, too, is contested, e.g., by R. Bultmann, *The History of the Synoptic Tradition* (ET, 1963), 295f. and 440.
[3] Luke 2.1–20, and on this Dibelius, 'Jungfrauensohn', 9ff.   [4] Matt. 1–2.
[5] On the much-discussed problem of the genealogical tree, cf. for recent works J. Jeremias, *Jerusalem zur Zeit Jesu* 2 (1958[2]), 154–68; M. Lambertz, 'Die Toledoth in Matt. 1.1–17 und Lukas 3.23ff.' in *Festschrift Franz Dornseiff* (1953), 201–25; O. Cullmann, *The Christology of the New Testament* (ET, 1959), 127–30; J. Schmid, 'Abstammung Marias', *LMK* I 1, 33f.; A. Vögtle, 'Genealogien', *LTK* 4, 661f.
[6] Matt. 1.16; Luke 3.23.
[7] But even today it is often adduced. On earlier attempts to come to terms with the contradictory genealogical tradition, cf., e.g., W. Bauer, *Das Leben Jesu im Zeitalter der neutestamentlichen Apokryphen* (1909), 21–29; A. Meyer and W. Bauer, 'The Relatives of Jesus' in E. Hennecke and W. Schneemelcher, *New Testament Apocrypha* I: Gospels and Related Writings (ET, 1963), 418ff.

were not originally drawn up by the evangelists and do not agree with each other, it means that we again have here two early witnesses who do not seem to be aware of the virgin birth, and who testify to Joseph as Jesus' natural father. It makes no difference for us whether we like to regard the genealogical assertions in themselves as old and 'historical' or as legendary and valueless; but the later one places them, the clearer they themselves make it that the tradition of the virgin birth was at first propagated and believed only within limited circles.

But even without this evidence it is obvious how the matter stood. This is shown by the rest of the New Testament. In Mark's Gospel the introductory story contains no reference at all to the virgin birth. The 'beginning of the gospel of Jesus Christ'[1] is given here with the appearance of John the Baptist, who was foretold by the prophet,[2] and to him 'Jesus came from Nazareth of Galilee' to be baptized.[3] As far as the *Heilsgeschichte* is concerned, everything that precedes this event is quite unimportant; but it is not on that account hidden and unknown. Jesus' home, occupation, and family relationships are no secret. It is precisely their indisputable ordinariness that is alleged to have stood in his way: 'Is not this the carpenter, the son of Mary and brother of James and Joses and Judas and Simon, and are not his sisters here with us?'[4] In that enumeration Jesus' father is not mentioned at all; and as reference is expressly made to relatives still living in the place, it may be assumed that he was dead. By those questions the 'many'[5] do not mean to reproach him with illegitimate parentage;[6] otherwise Jesus' answer would lose its point: 'A prophet is not without honour, except in his own country, and among his own kin, and in his own house'[7]—that means that he gains no prestige, because he is not a stranger and

---

[1] Mark 1.1.
[2] Mark 1.2ff.
[3] Mark 1.9ff.
[4] Mark 6.3.
[5] Mark 6.2: οἱ πολλοί. There is no need here to go into the fact that our *pericope* is not a unity, but only 'incongruous fragments' fitted together 'from a varying tradition': E. Lohmeyer, *Das Evangelium des Markus* (1954¹³), 110.
[6] Nor do 'the strict laws of the Jewish system of name-giving', to which E. Stauffer refers in *Jesus and his Story* (ET, 1960), 24f., 166, affect the matter at all. A son is named after his father as a matter of course, and only in case of illegitimacy after his unmarried mother; but the remarks of the Nazareth crowd are not a record of births.
[7] Mark 6.4.

'from afar', because he lacks the nimbus of the unknown, and not because people are aware of some secret stain that he bears. If the latter is what Mark had meant, he would have had to express himself more clearly and would not have passed over the reproach without dealing with it. Least of all can he have had the virgin birth in mind, as he is silent about it, and no unprejudiced reader would have understood that there was any allusion to it. Moreover the later tradition relating to this passage, which at first lacked the name and was apparently quite free of any overtones, added the father to it.[1] This completion appears in Matthew's Gospel,[2] and made its way, probably from there, into part of the Marcan tradition.[3] Luke, who reconstructed and greatly changed the whole *pericope*, even names Joseph alone.[4] Thus we see that something has arisen in contradiction to the stories of the miraculous birth, which both the evangelists took from another source. Unless, as is probable, it remained quite unnoticed, Matthew and Luke may, of course, have found a way out, as did later exegetes, by assuming that the Jews, who are the people speaking here, either did not know the facts about Jesus' parentage or would not acknowledge them, and that they therefore wrongly regarded his foster-father as his real father. (We can recognize from such divergences, which can also be noticed in other passages,[5] the literary relation of the introductory stories to the old corpus of the Marcan tradition into which they were brought.) In any case, we have no right to assume any such reflections for Mark, who nowhere mentions the virgin birth. The assertion that he must nevertheless have been aware of it and silently taken it into account is nothing but a glaring *petitio principii*.

In John's Gospel things are more difficult and more interesting. It is clear from the first that his text neither mentions nor in any way assumes the virgin birth. According to the explicit evidence that Philip gives in the very first chapter, Jesus is 'the son of Joseph'

---

[1] It may be that Joseph's name was not known at all in the oldest tradition.

[2] Matt. 13.55.

[3] If this less well attested Marcan tradition should be original, as, e.g., E. Klostermann, *Das Markusevangelium* (1950⁴), 55, and G. Bornkamm, *Jesus of Nazareth* (ET, 1960), 199, consider possible, the matter would be even simpler: the omission of the father would be a subsequent correction made in view of the virgin birth.

[4] Luke 4.22.

[5] A similar tension exists between Jesus' words in Luke 11.27f. and the statements in the hymns in Luke 1.42, 48, about his mother.

and comes from Nazareth.[1] It is not open to doubt that in the evangelist's mind these statements are correct and are to be taken seriously, for in continuing his presentation he comes back to them and never disavows them. Above all he shows—more than the synoptists—a fundamental, as it were negatively theological, interest in this aspect of Jesus' earthly existence. The true decision of faith must come from meeting Jesus and his testimony, in view of the ineffaceable double significance of his earthly person, without the help of miraculous phenomena and 'signs'. Anyone who, to avoid being offended by his lowliness, demands supporting evidence first, can never look on the present glory of the Revealer. This is the fundamental thought of the Gospel, and from it the question of Jesus' origin receives its light. The Jews demand from their Messiah something special and external, and they reject Jesus because he does not fulfil that expectation. They are concerned with proof of descent from David and with the promised Bethlehem origin;[2] they assert that if Jesus had really come from heaven, his parents could not be known to anyone.[3] Faith, however, discerns behind and in the unlikely reality of the One become flesh the glory of the only Son,[4] and it is in him that it finds the Father.[5]

It might, indeed, be theoretically possible to imagine that, just as Jesus can in the evangelist's opinion quite well fulfil, and on occasion does fulfil, the signs that are wrongly demanded,[6] he might, in fact, conform to the expectations as to his origin, and that the Jews simply would not have it so. This, however, is nowhere stated, and so we must again infer that in the evangelist's opinion it was not the case. Although he may have left open the question of descent from David,[7] the fact that he comes from despised Nazareth[8]

[1] John 1.45: εὑρίσκει Φίλιππος τὸν Ναθαναὴλ καὶ λέγει αὐτῷ· ὃν ἔγραψεν Μωϋσῆς ἐν τῷ νόμῳ καὶ οἱ προφῆται εὑρήκαμεν, Ἰησοῦν υἱὸν τοῦ Ἰωσὴφ τὸν ἀπὸ Ναζαρέθ.

[2] John 7.42: οὐχ ἡ γραφὴ εἶπεν ὅτι ἐκ σπέρματος Δαυὶδ καὶ ἀπὸ Βηθλέεμ τῆς κώμης ὅπου ἦν Δαυίδ, ἔρχεται ὁ Χριστός;

[3] John 6.42: οὐχ οὗτός ἐστιν Ἰησοῦς ὁ υἱὸς Ἰωσήφ, οὗ ἡμεῖς οἴδαμεν τὸν πατέρα καὶ τὴν μητέρα; πῶς νῦν λέγει ὅτι ἐκ οὐρανοῦ καταβέβηκα;

Characteristically, the mention of the mother has been deleted in some MSS, 'because the existence of a mother did not in the eyes of the' (later) 'Christians exclude the heavenly origin': W. Bauer, *Das Johannesevangelium* (1933³), 97.

[4] John 1.14.   [5] John 1.18; 14.8f.

[6] On this see, e.g., R. Bultmann, *Das Evangelium des Johannes* (1941), 152ff.

[7] It is not discussed at any length in John 7.42, and it is joined to the Bethlehem birth so as to stress the latter.

[8] John 1.46; cf. 7.41ff.

and from Galilee remains quite unshaken.[1] In contrast to the tendentious, apologetic legends in Matthew's and Luke's Gospels, John does not let go the humble reality of Jesus' origin, but gives it theological significance just as it is, a cause of offence and scandal. Or was he quite ignorant of the contrary Bethlehem tradition? That, in view of the age of such a tradition, is in my opinion hardly credible.[2] It is more likely that he purposely ignored it. If that is so, the relevant question as to Jesus' ancestry suggests itself at once. It is clear that John himself regards Joseph as Jesus' father. Did he therefore know nothing about the assertion of his miraculous origin, or is not the rejection of alleged Jewish expectations of which he writes really directed from the first against Christian legends, or at least partly against them?

The claim, at first sight surprising, that a heavenly revealer must not have had either father or mother, may remind us of corresponding docetic legends handed down to us from the second century;[3] their early forms certainly go back as far as John's Gospel itself. On the other hand, one verse of the prologue seems already to allude directly to the virgin-birth legend, which no doubt originated in the first century. It speaks of those who 'believed in his name', who 'received' Jesus, and who had thereby received 'power to become children of God', and as such 'were born, not of blood nor of the will of the flesh nor of the will of man, but of God'.[4] This declaration obviously aims in the first place at setting out in a quite general way the miraculous, 'supernatural' origin of the Christian nature, which can be neither explained nor achieved through earthly parentage or kinship.[5] Thus the Gospel later emphasizes the fact that even Jesus' brothers were not able to 'believe' in him;[6] it also

---

[1] John 7.52. W. Michaelis, 'Die Davidsohnschaft Jesu als historisches und kerygmatisches Problem' in H. Ristow and K. Matthiae, *Der historische Jesus und der kerygmatische Christus* (1961, pp. 317–30), 328ff., proceeds in the exposition of this text from assumptions that do not appear in John's Gospel itself, and so he has, it seems to me, completely misunderstood it.

[2] So, too, K. Stendahl, 'Quis et Unde? An Analysis of Mt. 1–2' in *Judentum, Urchristentum, Kirche* (Jeremias-Festschrift, BZNW 26, 1960, pp. 94–105), 97, n. 15.

[3] See p. 22 below.

[4] John 1.12f.: ὅσοι δὲ ἔλαβον αὐτόν, ἔδωκεν αὐτοῖς ἐξουσίαν τέκνα Θεοῦ γενέσθαι, τοῖς πιστεύουσιν εἰς τὸ ὄνομα αὐτοῦ, οἳ οὐκ ἐξ αἱμάτων οὐδὲ ἐκ θελήματος σαρκὸς οὐδὲ ἐκ θελήματος ἀνδρός, ἀλλ' ἐκ Θεοῦ ἐγεννήθησαν.

[5] Cf. Mark 3.31–35 parr.

[6] John 7.5; cf. 7.10.

describes the incomprehension of his mother, with whom Jesus will therefore have nothing to do at the decisive moment of the beginning of his ministry;[1] and thus the Jews' right to be called children of Abraham is denied in spite of their undoubted physical ancestry. [2]Natural parentage therefore does not determine spiritual nature; this is a typical Johannine idea which persistently recurs. But was it therefore necessary, even on his first preliminary appearance in the prologue, to put such stress on the contrasting natural physical parentage, to write in different words no less than three times about the nature of a natural birth, and to trace the birth back to 'the will of man'? All this, it is said, is of no account in the birth of the children of God. Thus the idea of a 'virgin birth' is forced on us at once; and where anything of that kind is known, the reader must be surprised to meet the idea used only in a purely figurative way that envisages all Christians. The history of the text also shows here that this obstacle is not merely modern, but that even in the earliest period, as soon as anything was known of the virgin birth, it brought difficulty and perplexity. Even in the second century people had begun to correct the verse and change the original plural into a singular—that is, to relate it directly to Christ himself and to his creation and birth taken in a physical sense. This correction certainly involves a misunderstanding, and perhaps not the original text;[3] but it seems to me that that misunderstanding might very well not rest on pure chance, but that the association with the idea of Jesus' virgin birth was intended all along. That would, in fact, mean that we should here have to do with a polemical allusion; for a virgin birth in the literal sense, as others had asserted it as regards Jesus, is rather, through the extension of the idea to Christians as a whole, robbed of its meaning and repudiated. Just as natural descent from Abraham does not prevent the children of Abraham from being described, not as such, but as children of the devil, so the believers, without prejudice to their natural procreation

[1] John 2.4.
[2] John 8.37–42.
[3] Against this opinion, which is still represented by F. M. Braun, 'Qui ex deo natus est (Jean 1.13)' in *Mélanges M. Goguel* (1950), 11–31, see most recently A. Houssiau, 'Le milieu théologique de la leçon ΕΓΕΝΝΗΘΗ (Joh. 1.13)' in F. Coppens and others, *Sacra pagina* 2 (1959), 170–98. 'One can only be surprised that devotional practice and dogmatic requirement have not carried the change through over a wider range', as Dibelius rightly says, 'Jung-frauensohn', p. 18, n. 22.

and birth through an earthly father and mother, are to be regarded as pure 'children of God', 'of virgin birth' like God's only Son[1]— who yet had Joseph as his father.

Unfortunately this problem cannot be decided with certainty. Most critical exegetes see in the verse in question no allusion to the virgin birth, and try to explain it by other analogies from the comparative study of religions.[2] The answer depends in some degree on when and where John's Gospel is supposed to have originated. But however that may be, this Gospel is in any case a clear witness against the supposedly general acknowledgment of the virgin birth in primitive Christian preaching as a whole. Mark and John stand over against the infancy stories in Matthew and Luke; and almost all primitive Christian literature confirms by its silence that the 'doctrine' of the virgin birth was foreign to it, or at least a matter of secondary importance or indifference. We must now briefly enlarge on this.

Of course, the *argumentum e silentio* must not be pressed in relation to an isolated text or document; it may be that in one case or another the silence is a matter of pure chance. But as regards Paul such qualifications are not relevant; his legacy is too big for that, and too rich in Christological assertions and formulae. It is true that the badly overworked text of Gal. 4.4, taken alone as it stands, is not clear evidence against the virgin birth.[3] That Paul here writes of the Son of God as born of a 'woman' is simply to emphasize the abasement to share the common lot of all mankind; that is how Christ was able to bestow kinship with God on all who are born of

---

[1] A similar point of view can perhaps also be found in the *Acta Pilati* 1.1; 2.3–6; 16.2; thus F. Scheidweiler in Hennecke and Schneemelcher, *NT Apocrypha* I, 444ff.

[2] Cf. Bultmann, *Johannesevangelium*, 38, n. 2; J. H. Waszink, art. 'Embryologie' II B in *RAC* IV, 1241f. Orthodox and Catholic exponents try to appraise the passage as positive evidence for the virgin birth; e.g. T. Zahn, *Das Evangelium des Johannes* (1908), 75f.; P. Botz, O.S.B., *Die Jungfrauenschaft Mariens im Neuen Testament und in der nachapostolischen Zeit* (Diss. theol. Tübingen, 1935), 14, and with reservations C. K. Barrett, *The Gospel according to St John* (1955), 137f. The question becomes further complicated if, like C. C. Torrey, 'The Aramaic Origin of the Gospel of John', *HTR* 16 (1923, pp. 305–44), 328, we take into account Aramaic sources in the relevant passage, and then perhaps regard the reference to the Christians instead of to Jesus as simply a mistake in translation, 'a very disturbing mistranslation': Torrey, *The Four Gospels—a New Translation* (1947), 316.

[3] Gal. 4.4: . . . ἐξαπέστειλεν ὁ Θεὸς τὸν υἱὸν αὐτοῦ, γενόμενον ἐκ γυναικός, γενόμενον ὑπὸ νόμον . . .

woman. In such a context 'woman' does not imply a contrast with 'virgin', but simply denotes in a general way the nature of genera- tion, to originate from which is the mark of all human beings, who from birth are indeed of anything but divine race.[1] But we can see from this text how little room the Pauline two-stage Christology leaves for the idea of a virgin birth; in the pattern of abasement and exaltation the 'birth' means the lowest point of self-stripping. For Paul everything hangs on the fact that Christ really became in all respects like men 'under the law' whom he redeems. 'If the text read "γενόμενον ἐκ παρθένου", born of a virgin, the words would be stripped of their meaning.'[2] With Paul this does not occur only in this one passage; when he comes to speak, in language that was already traditional, of the Lord's descent and ascension, the virgin birth is absent, as in good sense it must be absent.[3] Once, in the introductory passage of Romans, Paul mentions—as it were to show his orthodoxy—the Lord's kinship with David, which plays no part elsewhere in his thinking; but even here he says nothing about the virgin birth.[4] All this can hardly fail to lead to the conclusion that he knew of no such theological doctrine. In any case, generation 'according to the Spirit' is not thought of in his writings, even remotely, as a physiological miracle.[5] In this he was certainly no exception. There is nothing to indicate that, for example, the letters composed later under his name, or the other writings of the New Testament, knew and put forward anything more than he did in this matter.

[1] Cf., e.g., Job 14.1; Matt. 11.11 = Luke 7.28. T. Zahn's attempt, in *Der Brief des Paulus an die Galater* (1923³), 201f., to make this text, too, a piece of indirect evidence for the virgin birth because no father is mentioned needs no refutation. If that kind of interpretation were in any sense natural, Macbeth would no doubt have been saved from his error.

[2] Dibelius, 'Jungfrauensohn', p. 29, n. 47.

[3] Phil. 2.5-11. Since Lohmeyer's 'Kyrios Jesus', *Sitzungsberichte der Heidel- berger Akademie*, 1927/28, No. 4, it has been acknowledged that in this text Paul uses an older hymn.

[4] Rom. 1.3, and on it O. Kuss, *Der Römerbrief* (Lfg. 1, 1957), 5-9.

[5] Dibelius, 'Jungfrauensohn', 27ff., would certainly like to accept this. From Gal. 4.22-30 he infers that in this passage with Isaac in view Paul, like Philo, followed a Hellenistic-Jewish way of thinking, according to which in the 'miraculous begetting of one chosen by God, the creative Spirit takes the place of the begetting man' (p. 29). But this exposition cannot be maintained; cf. S. Lösch, *Deitas Jesu und antike Apotheose* (1933), 86ff.; Otto Michel and Otto Betz, 'Von Gott gezeugt' in *Judentum, Urchristentum, Kirche* (Jeremias- Festschrift, 1960, 3-23), 18. There are three reasons that tell especially against

But it is certainly not for the New Testament alone that this conclusion is valid. It seems to me that too little account is taken of the fact that all the so-called 'apostolic fathers'—with one important exception—do not seem to know of the virgin birth. At least in the *Letter of Barnabas* and the *Shepherd* of Hermas this cannot possibly be due to chance, for both of them develop quite detailed speculations about the Lord's origin and earthly form.[1] The exception is Bishop Ignatius of Antioch, the 'Bishop of Syria' as he calls himself.[2] Ignatius lays great theological stress on the virgin birth, and already regards it as an indispensable doctrine that has been handed down, and to which he refers in formal, almost confessional, language. We shall have to discuss his ideas later.[3] The point here is that with it we are again landed in the same geographical area from which Matthew's Gospel and the Lucan sources of the infancy narratives may have first come. No other fragments of Christian writings up to the middle of the second century that have been handed down to us speak of the virgin birth.[4] We find it again—once more in the set phrases of confessional formulae—when we come to Justin, who came from Machusa near Flavia Neapolis, the old Sichem in Palestine, again from Palestinian-Syrian territory. It therefore looks as if the legend

---

these writers: (1) in the parallel passage Rom. 4.18–21 Isaac is declared to be Abraham's son; (2) the contrast κατὰ σάρκα — κατὰ πνεῦμα is not used by Paul elsewhere in the sense 'physical, bodily' and 'spiritual'; and (3) most important, the quotation from Isa. 54.1 in Gal. 4.27 is to be related not, as Dibelius would have it, to Sarah, but clearly to 'Jerusalem'. Here too, therefore, the assertion of a 'spiritual' birth does not envisage the elimination of the man.

[1] Cf. the complete collation in the supplement to Lietzmann's *Handbuch zum Neuen Testament: Die Apostolischen Väter*. On Barnabas, H. Windisch, p. 374f.: how Barnabas 'imagined the birth is difficult to say. . . . He will not even allow that he who appeared in the flesh is the son of a human being, 12. 10.' 'For him the main difficulty of Christology is in the question how the heavenly Father could assume flesh and even accept suffering for himself'. On Hermas, Dibelius, pp. 572–6: the 'coming together of different substances' is emphasized and a pneumatic Christology developed, which does not, however, succeed in reaching a clear conclusion, because 'the significant motive for pneumatic Christology, the single and unique incarnation of a divine Being in Jesus Christ, does not come about.' On Hermas cf. also Peter Knorz, *Die Theologie des 'Hirten des Hermas'* (Diss. theol. Heidelberg, 1958, typewritten), 53ff.

[2] Ign. *Rom.* 2.2.

[3] See pp. 29f. below.

[4] We may certainly refer here to the *Apology* of Aristides 'of Athens' (Eusebius, *Chronicon ad annum Abr.* 2140 = A.D. 125). We have here in the Greek text 15.1: οὗτος δὲ ὁ υἱὸς τοῦ Θεοῦ τοῦ ὑψίστου ὁμολονεῖται ἐν πνεύματι ἁγίω

were born and bred in that district.[1] Unless all the indications are deceptive, it was given more general circulation through being read in Matthew's and Luke's Gospels. With these Gospels it became more and more widely known,[2] and on account of this biblical testimony the virgin birth was at last accepted and belief in it was made obligatory.[3]

Justin himself may have already read Matthew's and Luke's Gospels; but he assigns them no 'canonical' importance, and never expressly takes his stand on their text. He does not yet venture,

---

ἀπ' οὐρανοῦ καταβὰς [διὰ τὴν σωτηρίαν τῶν ἀνθρώπων] καὶ ἐκ παρθένου [ἁγίας γεννηθεὶς ἀσπόρως τε καὶ ἀφθόρως] σάρκα ἀνέλαβε . . . The words in brackets are rightly regarded as additions of the Barlaam story, which goes further than the Syriac which, as the accompanying Greek fragment shows, likewise paraphrases very freely: R. Seeberg, 'Die Apologie des Aristides, untersucht und wiederhergestellt', in T. Zahn, *Forschungen zur Geschichte des neutestamentlichen Kanons* 5 (1893), 171, 330; J. Geffcken, *Zwei griechische Apologeten* (1907), 83f.; Hugo Koch, *Virgo Eva—Virgo Maria* (1937), 76, n. 1. Accordingly it is on no account admissible, in mistaken reliance on the Armenian tradition, to follow G. Söll, *LMK* I 2 (1958) in quoting Aristides as the first witness to use the epithet 'holy' about Mary. But the whole text of the *Apology* is questionable, and should be used only with the greatest caution. Today the problem with which it confronts us is 'presented afresh', as C. Andresen rightly emphasizes, art. 'Aristides' in *RGG* I, 597. How easily corrections can appear in formal dogmatic contexts is shown, e.g., in the corresponding passage in the text of the Third Letter to the Corinthians in the *Acta Pauli*: Koch, *op. cit.*, p. 67, n. 1. Above all, however, the origin and temporal setting of the text is anything but certain, *pace* R. M. Grant, 'The Chronology of the Greek Apologists', *Vigiliae Christianae* 9 (1955, pp. 25–33), 25. According to G. C. O'Ceallaigh, ' "Marcianus" Aristides, On the Worship of God',*HTR* 51 (1958), 227–54, it is a fourth-century elaboration of an originally Jewish apology. One cannot build on evidence that can be contested on so many grounds.

[1] John's Gospel, or at least part of its sources, also belongs to this locality. That is important in judging the questionable 'evidence' of John 1.13 (see p. 16 above).
[2] It seems that the Cerinthians and Ebionites, who used Matthew's Gospel (Irenaeus, *Haer.* I 26.1f.), but nevertheless opposed belief in the virgin birth, had to delete the first chapter and in any case change the genealogical tree: Epiphanius, *Haer.* XXVIII 5.1; XXX 14.13; cf. XXIX 9.4. On the alterations of the Syriac Bible see p. 23 below.
[3] Beside these we can point to the creeds or creed-like formulae that are already recognizable in Ignatius—still without invoking the Gospel writings: H. Köster, *Synoptische Überlieferung bei den apostolischen Vätern* (1957), 6of. But as bearers of the virgin birth idea they are no doubt less important after the consolidation of the canon. In themselves they are hardly able to mediate a particular 'theology' of the virgin birth, but for their interpretation other sources, too, must at times be tapped; cf. J. J. Carpenter, 'The Birth from Holy Spirit and the Virgin in the Old Roman Creed', *JTS* 40 (1939), 31–36.

therefore, simply to object to the name 'Christian' in the case of such Christians as reject the virgin birth. In his dialogue with the Jew Trypho he consciously recognizes different degrees of theological importance between the fundamental faith, on which all Christians must stand firm, that Jesus is the Christ, and the further assertions about Christ's pre-existence and virgin birth.[1] Justin knows that there are Jewish Christians who indeed confess Jesus as Messiah, but who at the same time maintain that his birth was a natural one; and although he disapproves of the latter opinion, he contents himself with the certainty that most Christians who were at one with him thought as he did on this point.[2] In my opinion he must in this passage[3] have had in mind as an exception not only out-and-out heretics, with whom he realizes that he is no longer in company;[4] it is rather a question of Hellenistic Christians, who are in the same community as he. It is obvious that even in the camp of the orthodox there is still a good deal of latitude with regard to the doctrine of Christ's incarnation.

In the following period this latitude rapidly diminished. With Irenaeus, who solemnly affirms the canon of the four Gospels,[5] the virgin birth has already become an essential part of Christian doctrine,[6] and since then the opposing view of 'Ebion' and the Ebionites has been regarded as wicked and blasphemous heresy.[7] Jewish Christianity became a sect under this name. But the same kind of thing, of course, is true for the deviating tenets of the

---

[1] *Dial.* 48.2f.: ἤδη μέντοι, ὦ Τρύφων, εἶπον, οὐκ ἀπόλλυται τὸ τοῦτον εἶναι Χριστὸν τοῦ Θεοῦ, ἐὰν ἀποδεῖξαι μὴ δύνωμαι ὅτι καὶ προυπῆρχεν υἱὸς τοῦ ποιητοῦ τῶν ὅλων, Θεὸς ὤν, καὶ γεγένηται ἄνθρωπος, διὰ τῆς παρθένου κτλ.; cf. *Dial.* 68.

[2] *Dial.* 48.4: καὶ γὰρ εἰσί τινες, ὦ φίλοι, ἔλεγον, ἀπὸ τοῦ ὑμετέρου γένους ὁμολογοῦντες αὐτὸν Χριστὸν εἶναι, ἄνθρωπον δὲ ἐξ ἀνθρώπων γενόμενον ἀποφαινόμενοι· οἷς οὐ συντίθεμαι, οὐδ' ἂν πλεῖστοι ταῦτά μοι δοξάσαντες εἴποιεν, ἐπειδὴ οὐκ ἀνθρωπείοις διδάγμασι κεκελεύσμεθα ὑπ' αὐτοῦ τοῦ Χριστοῦ πείθεσθαι, ἀλλὰ τοῖς διὰ τῶν μακαρίων προφητῶν κηρυχθεῖσι καὶ δι' αὐτοῦ διδαχθεῖσι.

[3] οὐδ' ἂν πλεῖστοι ταῦτά μοι δοξάσαντες εἴποιεν: cf. the various attempts at translation in J. C. T. Otto, *Justini philosophi et martyris opera* I 2 (1877), 164, n. 12.

[4] *Apol.* I 26.

[5] *Haer.* III 11.8f.

[6] See pp. 23ff. below.

[7] See, e.g., A. v. Harnack, *Lehrbuch der Dogmengeschichte* I (1931⁴), 317ff. (ET of 3rd ed., *History of Dogma* I, 1894, 294ff.), and the listing of anti-Ebionite controversialists in H. J. Schoeps, *Theologie und Geschichte des Judenchristentums* (1949), 73, n. 2. J. Daniélou, *Théologie du Judéo-Christianisme* (Tournai, 1958), does not investigate this branch of Jewish Christianity and passes over the problems involved in it.

Gnostics.[1] With regard to the virgin birth, these people either agree with the Jewish Christians, and assert that according to his physical origin (only according to this, of course!) Jesus was a natural human being, the son of Joseph and Mary[2]—or develop a purely docetic Christology, which means that they see in Christ a supramundane being like an angel, who has no earthly nature, but who, as Marcion taught, came down direct from heaven in the form of a grown-up man in the fifteenth year of the principate of Tiberius.[3] We must not regard these views as entirely secondary and directed against the doctrine of the virgin birth; they are, on the contrary, further evidence of how little the virgin birth was taken as a matter of course, even at the beginning and up to the middle of the second century.[4] Probably neither Cerdo nor Cerinthus, neither Satornilus nor the Carpocratians, perhaps not even Marcion, held the opinion that their Christological doctrines contradicted a well-established tradition. Right into the third century there are not only Jewish Christian but also Gentile Christian groups that maintain that Jesus was begotten naturally, and, as Origen complains, will not believe that the Lord was born of a virgin.[5]

It is even more characteristic that the resistance to the new

[1] On what follows cf. the convenient summary in Walter Bauer, *Das Leben Jesu*, 29–58. The numerous recent discoveries and publications have not changed in its essentials the sketch given here. I do not go into details of gnostic doctrines as they would need a separate investigation. The Holy Spirit may appear as Jesus' mother (*Gospel according to the Hebrews, Letter of James* in the Jung Codex); Mary is regarded as an angel (*Gospel according to the Hebrews*); or Christ is regarded as the angel Gabriel or Michael, who enters into her (*Epistola apostolorum, Pistis Sophia*), cf. J. Michel, Art. 'Engel III (gnostisch)' in *RAC* V (cols. 97–109), 107f. However, the history of gnostic doctrines about Jesus' parentage goes far beyond ancient times: cf. Arno Borst, *Die Katharer* (1953), 162–7.

[2] So Cerinthus: Iren. *Haer.* I 26.1; Hippolyt. *Ref.* VII 33.1; the Carpocratians: Iren. *Haer.* 1 25.1; Justin the Gnostic: Hippol. *Ref.* V 26.29; also the *Gospel of Philip* 17.91; the *Acts of Thomas* 2. For the exposition of the *Gospel of Thomas* 15, cf. Bertil Gärtner, *The Theology of the Gospel according to Thomas* (1961), 84f.

[3] So Cerdo: Hippol. *Ref.* VII 31; Epiphan. *Haer.* XLI 1.7; Satornilus: Iren. *Haer.* I 24.2; Monoimus: Hippol. *Ref.* VIII 13.3; Marcion: Tert. *Adv. Marc.* I 15.19; III 11; IV 7.21; Hippol. *Ref.* VII 31; cf. Epiphan. *Haer.* XXX 13.2f.; probably also Tatian: Theodoret, *Haeret. fab. comp.* I 20; on this M. Elze, *Tatian und seine Theologie* (1960), 124f.; cf. R. M. Grant, 'The heresy of Tatian', *JTS*, NS 5 (1954, pp. 62–68), 65f.

[4] Similarly W. Bousset, *Kyrios Christos* (1921²), 213f., 269.

[5] *Comm. Mt.* XVI 12 (Klostermann, p. 513): . . . τοὺς ἀπὸ τῶν ἐθνῶν, οἵτινες παρ' ὀλίγους ἅπαντες πεπιστεύκασιν αὐτὸν ἐκ παρθένου γεγενῆσθαι.

doctrine of the virgin birth is nowhere specially unyielding. Only the conservative Marcionites and later the Manicheans hold strictly to the old docetic tradition and reject any kind of birth for Christ. The Valentinians, on the other hand, took over the virgin birth without difficulty with the Gospels of the great Church, and, later at any rate, they taught it generally. They contented themselves with an interpretation of it that conformed to their own views[1] by asserting that Christ nevertheless took to himself nothing earthly from Mary, but had passed through her like water through a pipe or channel[2]—an idea that Irenaeus very properly recognized as entirely docetic,[3] but which agreed admirably with the acceptance of a virgin birth. In time the doctrine of the virgin birth finds its way in even among the Ebionites;[4] so for Jewish Christians, too, it did not by any means constitute the decisive point of antagonism to the Catholic Church as a whole. The same is true of the Christological theories of the adoptionists, in whose eyes the spiritual nature of Jesus is based, not on his birth, but on his baptism;[5] they, too, have no difficulty in upholding the biblical doctrine of the virgin birth. Attempts to modify the text of the birth stories can in some measure be conclusively proved only in regard to Syria, and they play no essential part.[6]

This means that the preaching of the virgin birth is, in a certain sense, not aligned to all the theological controversies and debates that fill the second century and even the period following. In the

[1] The Sethians, for example, do that in another way: Hippol. *Ref.* V 19.20, and the Naassenes: *Ref.* V 6.6f.

[2] Iren. *Haer.* III 11.3: 'quasi aquam per tubum', ὥσπερ ὕδωρ διὰ σωλῆνος; Ps. Tert. *haer.* 4.5: 'quasi aquam per fistulam'. This formula is repeatedly quoted by controversialists: H. J. Schoeps, *Vom himmlischen Fleisch Christi* (1951) 6. The later Bardesanites agreed in this with the Valentinians: Walter Bauer, *Rechtgläubigkeit und Ketzerei im ältesten Christentum* (1934), 36. Similarly the 'Gnostics' in Epiphanius, *Haer.* XXVI 10.5.

[3] Iren. *Haer.* III 22.1; V 1.2.

[4] Cf. Harnack, *Dogmengeschichte* I 321ff. (ET, I, 299ff.). Among the gnosticizing Elkesaites the virgin birth had its place beside other possibilities: Hippol. *Ref.* IX 14.1; X 29.2. That may also have been the case elsewhere more often than we think.

[5] So, for instance, in Theodotus of Byzantium: Hippol. *Ref.* X 23.

[6] I am thinking here of the famous related variants of the Vetus Syra on Matt. 1.16, 21, 25; Luke 2.4, 5. Though they certainly do not give the original text, they give corrections that must go back into the second century, and which then, as Heinrich Greeven has kindly pointed out to me, can probably be understood only in the sense of Joseph's natural paternity.

anti-gnostic front the Catholic fathers, too, are interested above all,[1] not really in the virgin birth, but in the reality of an actual fully human birth; and with regard to Jews, Jewish Christians, and 'adoptionists' they are, on the contrary, concerned above all with the pre-temporal 'birth' of the Son—that is, with the problem of his pre-existence, but again not with his birth from a virgin. The fact is that the doctrine of the virgin birth was not formulated for the sake of a theological line of thought; it is simply a supposedly 'apostolic' piece of biblical tradition that was handed down. It was not defence, but interpretation, with which the early Church saw itself confronted in relation to this piece of doctrine.

[1] 'Above all'—but not exclusively. It is going too far when F. Lau, in *TLZ* 86 (1961), 512, expresses the summary opinion that 'in the early Church Jesus' birth from the Holy Spirit and the Virgin Mary was proof, not of his true divinity, but of his true humanity'. That can be said at the most with regard to Mary, who must, in fact, first guarantee Jesus' 'humanity', so that the miracle of virginity recedes; but in no case can it be said of the Holy Spirit, who can testify only to the Saviour's divine origin. Later, however, even the birth from the Virgin was made a mark of divine origin; in fact, with this implication it becomes contrasted with mere carnal birth; cf. the *Tome* (= *Ep.* 28.4) of Leo the Great (Schwartz, *Acta conc. oecum.* II 2, p. 28): 'nativitas carnis manifestatio est humanae naturae, partus virginis divinae est virtutis indicium'. The first evidence of this assessment comes from Lactantius, *Inst.* IV 12 ('. . . . illo per virginem nato confiteri homines oportebat deum secum esse, id est in terra et in carne mortali'), and Eusebius of Caesarea, *Demonstr.* IV 10.20: τικτόμενος μὲν ἡμῶν ὁμοίως, καὶ θνητοῦ δίκην ἄνθρωπον ἀμφιεννύμενος, ὡς δ' οὐκέτι ἄνθρωπος, ἀλλὰ Θεός, ἐξ ἀχράντου καὶ ἀπειρογάμου κόρης οὐχὶ δὲ ἐκ μίξεως καὶ φθορᾶς, τὴν τοῦ φαινομένου γένεσιν ὑφιστάμενος. This point of view appears clearly in Athanasius; see also p. 63, n. 4 below.

II

The Virgin Birth in
Apologetic and Dogma

THE STARTING-POINT of all later exposition of the virgin birth
is, of course, the two oldest accounts in the New Testament itself,
namely the annunciation scene in Luke's Gospel,[1] and the homo-
geneous introductory sketch in Matthew.[2] That is therefore where
we must begin with our presentation.

The idea that the virgin birth obviously represents a completely
miraculous act of God, with which the sending of the Saviour and
Messiah into the world begins, is common to both evangelists. But
it is only in *Luke* that the inner relation of this event to the nature
of the child so born is expressly brought out and stressed: just
because no human being, no man, but the Holy Spirit, will come
over Mary and 'overshadow' her,[3] the 'holy' one thus born will be
called the Son of God.[4] Doubts of the possibility of such an event
are expressly dismissed: just Elizabeth has conceived a son in her
old age, so God can now bring about an even greater miracle, birth
from a virgin; for with him 'nothing will be impossible'.[5] On Mary's
part the response to this divine action—and it is emphasized by the
contrasting picture of doubting Zechariah[6]—is simple and obedient[7]

---

[1] The remaining infancy stories, as mentioned above (pp. 10f.), are not set out
under the presupposition of the virgin birth, and so they provide nothing for its
interpretation.

[2] To all appearances they are independent of each other. That Luke has given
'an elaboration of St Matthew's design' is a completely unproved assertion by
P. J. Thompson, 'The Infancy Gospels of St Matthew and St Luke compared',
Studia Evangelica (TU 73, 1959), 217–22.

[3] As Dibelius, 'Jungfrauensohn', 19ff., has shown, the expression is no
'euphemism'. David Daube, 'Evangelisten und Rabbinen', *ZNW* 48 (1957,
pp. 119–26), 119ff., argues in favour of an Aramaic origin.

[4] Luke 1.35.   [5] Luke 1.36f.
[6] Luke 1.8–23.   [7] Luke 1.38.

acceptance in faith.[1] Thus as she has 'found favour with God',[2] she is 'the mother of my Lord'.[3] Because of this high favour she is called blessed,[4] although she is not on that account to be spared poignant grief.[5]

In *Matthew* the presentation takes a different form all along.[6] Here it is not a question of the story of the birth as such, nor of what the birth of the Son of God may mean in itself and for his mother. Matthew is concerned exclusively with the prophetic evidence, with the proof that Jesus really is, according to his origin and home, the expected Messiah, David's Son[7] and Emmanuel,[8] the Nazarene,[9] coming from Bethlehem[10] and called out of Egypt.[11] With all this the narrative takes on at the same time an apologetic character; with Joseph's doubt the polemic of the unbelieving Jews, too, is refuted. Holy Scripture shows that they are wrong, and in particular the virgin birth is proved, in accordance with Isa. 7.14 (in the LXX translation), to be a fixed part of the divine plan of salvation, and is made unassailable.

Thus Luke and Matthew look in different directions, and at times follow out a different purpose with their presentation. We can describe them briefly as the 'dogmatic' and the 'apologetic' line. These two directions will continue in subsequent theology. The apologetic exposition understands the virgin birth from the point of view of the *Heilsgeschichte*, as a sign of prophecy fulfilled; it proves that Jesus Christ as the Virgin's Son really is the prophesied Messiah and Redeemer; and thus it stands right in the old, historical tradition of Old Testament Jewish thought. On the other hand, the dogmatic exposition seems to go beyond that, and at the very least to touch on or handle a metaphysical question of substance and

---

[1] Luke 1.44.   [2] Luke 1.30.   [3] Luke 1.43.

[4] Luke 1.48. It may be interesting to note that this glorification is extended by Christ himself to Pilate in the apocryphal *Preaching of Pilate* 10 (C. Tischendorf, *Evangelia Apocrypha*[2] [1876], 455): μακαριοῦσίν σε πᾶσαι αἱ γενεαὶ καὶ αἱ πατριαὶ τῶν ἐθνῶν ὅτι ἐπί σου ἐπληρώθησαν ταῦτα πάντα τὰ ὑπὸ τῶν προφητῶν εἰρημένα περὶ ἐμοῦ.

[5] Luke 2.35. It is, moreover, worth noticing how consistently Mary is seen and understood in the Lucan infancy stories as a human 'figure', much more so than in all the following development—a point of view to which Herr Schadewaldt drew my attention in discussing this exposition.

[6] On what follows, cf. the excellent exposition by Krister Stendahl, 'Quis et unde? An Analysis of Mt. 1–2' in *Judentum, Urchristentum, Kirche*, 94–105.

[7] Matt. 1.20.   [8] Matt. 1.23, 25.   [9] Matt. 2.23.
[10] Matt. 2.6.   [11] Matt. 2.15.

nature. The angel's words of annunciation emphasize that the coming Saviour and Messiah will be called into life not through human, but solely through divine action, through 'the power of the Most High'.[1] God's Spirit has not merely awakened and filled him, but has ordained and begotten his earthly person even in the first act of his coming into being. To Jewish thinking that is certainly a completely foreign and surprising idea. At the same time it seems to me open to question whether it is therefore necessary to attribute it indirectly via Hellenistic Judaism, or indeed directly, to pagan mythological ideas, in which crude ideas of unions between gods and mortals were already surmounted and 'sublimated'.[2] The text itself, with its numerous biblical allusions, points rather in another direction; in fact, the stories about the 'forerunner' John the Baptist immediately preceding it obviously revive the pattern of the births of Old Testament promise-bearers and saviours—Isaac,[3] Samson,[4] and Samuel[5]—who are likewise miraculously born to old and barren women through the unexpected intervention of God.[6] The direct begetting by the Spirit from a virgin may appear from this angle as the fit and proper climax of the older theme, and one

---

[1] Luke 1.35.

[2] This is stressed (against Dibelius) by H. Braun, 'Der Sinn der neutestamentlichen Christologie', *ZTK* 54 (1957, 341–77), 354, n. 3. Here and elsewhere today Egyptian theology is specially in mind; cf. Emma Brunner-Traut, 'Die Geburtsgeschichte der Evangelien im Lichte der ägyptologischen Forschung', *ZRGG* 12 (1960), 97–111; the same: 'Pharao und Jesus als Söhne Gottes', *Antaios* 2 (1961), 266–84; Siegfried Schulz, art. ἐπισκιάζω' in *TWNT* VII, 403. But according to Siegfried Morenz 'the great Egyptian theology' has 'nothing to contribute' in regard to the real 'virgin birth': *Die Geschichte von Joseph dem Zimmermann* (1951), 56f. A Qumran origin of the idea of a virgin birth of the Messiah is discussed by Michel and Betz, 'Von Gott gezeugt', pp. 15f.; cf. also Matthew Black, *The Scrolls and Christian Origins* (1961), 81ff.

[3] Gen. 17.15–19; 18.9–16; 21.1–7. Luke 1.37 brings in a direct quotation from Gen. 18.14.

[4] Judg. 13.2–24.   [5] I Sam. 1.1–20.

[6] Cf. F. Dornseiff, 'Lukas der Schriftsteller', *ZNW* 35 (1936), 129ff. P. Winter, 'Some observations on the Language in the Birth and Infancy Stories of the Third Gospel', *Novum Testamentum* 1 (1956), 184–99, shows the effect of the Samson and Samuel stories in Pseudo-Philo, *Liber antiquitatum biblicarum*; cf. also R. McL. Wilson, 'Some Recent Studies in the Lucan Infancy Narratives,' *Studia Evangelica* (TU 73, 1959), 235–53. Later the same theme is taken up once more for the birth of Mary in the *Protevangelium of James* 1.3; 2.4, even with express reference to Sarah and Abraham. Reference to these Old Testament stories of surpassingly miraculous births is especially frequent in Chrysostom: cf., e.g., the homily entitled *Quod non oporteat peccata fratrum evulgare* (PG 51, 359ff.).

proportionate to the immeasurable significance of Jesus. But this question may be allowed to rest here.[1]

How Christ's divine and human 'nature' (in the Greek sense) are related to each other is not even distantly alluded to in the Gospel text, and is remote from it in character.[2] But in the Hellenistic world this problem will arise soon enough, and there will be no evading it. Something similar may be said of the part played by the 'virgin 'as mother in this connection. In Luke the one purport of her questions to the angel is to bring fully to light the significance of the unprecedented divine action.[3] That Mary has 'no husband'[4] is not a problem about which any further biographical or moral enlightenment is needed.[5] The intact virgin—not just any married woman—appears as the fit instrument of a miraculous divine begetting that needs no human or male participation. Whether and why it was necessary to eliminate the man in this connection (how else should a divine begetting be imagined at all?) and whether and why virginity might well form an essential presupposition of true divine maternity— such and similar questions are neither asked nor suggested by the evangelists. Matthew contents himself with the brief observation that Joseph did not know his wife till she had borne her son,[6] and all four evangelists agree straightforwardly that Jesus had brothers born of Mary's marriage after the coming of her 'first-born'[7]—that is, more sons (and daughters).[8] On this point, too, speculation will

[1] Nor am I going into the question, which has lately been much discussed, whether the (heterogeneous) sources that Luke uses were composed in Hebrew, Aramaic, or Greek. No really conclusive argument has yet been found in one case or the other for the origin of the ideas for which they are evidence.

[2] This is stressed, not without a certain one-sidedness, by F. Hahn, *Anfänge christologischer Traditionen* (Diss. theol. Heidelberg 1961, typewritten), 365ff.

[3] Most recently on this cf. J. Gewiess, 'Die Marienfrage, Lk. 1.34,' *Biblische Zeitschrift*, NF 5 (1961), 221–54.

[4] Luke 1.34.

[5] Mary's betrothal to Joseph is not original in the story of the annunciation, but became necessary only through its being combined with the nativity story, which shows Joseph and Mary as a married couple; cf. Dibelius, 'Jungfrauensohn', pp. 11f., 18; Bultmann, *Synoptic Tradition*, 295f. and 440. In Islam, too, Mary is regarded as an unaffianced girl, and the figure of Joseph is again (?) eliminated; cf. H. Stieglecker, *Die Glaubenslehren des Islam* II (1960), 252ff. In the latter part of the fourth century a certain Craterius was still trying to contest the fact of Mary's betrothal: Jerome, *Adv. Helv.* 3.16.

[6] Matt. 1.25.   [7] Luke 2.7.

[8] Jesus' brothers are mentioned in Matt. 12.46–48; 13.55; Mark 3.31–33; 6.3; Luke 8.19f.; John 2.12; 7.3, 5; Acts 1.14; I Cor. 9.5; Gal. 1.19; cf. T. Zahn,

in time set in and seek definite answers, which have prepared or made possible the consolidation of a special Marian doctrine. We first follow the chronological course of the development.

The first, and as we have seen, for a long time the only witness after Luke and Matthew for the virgin birth is Bishop *Ignatius* of Antioch, whose letters come from the second decade of the second century.[1] He is a convinced representative of the 'dogmatic' point of view. For Ignatius the virgin birth is a piece of the Church's recognized tradition, to which he refers in fixed phrases reminiscent of confessional formulae.[2] But that does not mean that this point of doctrine was merely part of his mental luggage;[3] it has its place in the centre of his conviction. The virgin birth is the very special sign of salvation in the Christian faith. Indeed, the whole of Ignatius's theology revolves round the great contrast between the human and the divine, the realm of death and the realm of life. It is on the fact that both have met in Christ, and that mortality has thus been translated into immortality, that our salvation rests. The primary miracle of redemption depends on the incarnation, on the paradoxical fact that Christ was both the Son of God and—in a new sense that expressly emphasizes the earthly aspect of his being— the Son of man, or, what comes to the same thing, that he is descended on the one side from the seed of David, but on the other from the Holy Spirit. The virgin birth in its incredibility is the given 'sign' of the paradoxical coming of salvation, surpassing in its significance even the passion, though the latter, too, is heavily stressed. For Ignatius there are three great realities in the plan of salvation, 'crying to be told, but wrought in God's silence': Mary's

---

'Brüder u. Vettern Jesu' in *Forschungen zur Geschichte des NT Kanons* . . . 6 (1900), 225–364; A. Meyer and W. Bauer, 'The Relatives of Jesus' in Hennecke and Schneemelcher, *NT Apocrypha* I, 418ff. In spite of the impressive expositions of J. Blinzler, 'Zum Problem der Brüder des Herrn', *Trierer Theologische Zeitschrift* 67 (1958), 129–45; 224–46, I do not want here to go again into the innumerable attempts to weaken or evade these pieces of evidence, but to stick to the 'simplest and most obvious' explanation (p. 134).

[1] The doubts expressed by H. Grégoire, *Les persécutions dans l'empire romain* (1951), 102ff., and again recently by Jacques Moreau, *Die Christenverfolgungen im römischen Reich* (1961), 45, n. 18, about the date and authenticity of the original Ignatian documents do not seem to me well founded.

[2] *Eph.* 7.2; 18.2; *Trall.* 9.1; *Smyrn.* 1.1.

[3] So H. Schlier, *Religionsgeschichtliche Untersuchungen zu den Ignatiusbriefen* (1929), 42f.

virginity (in the conception), the miracle of the birth, and 'likewise the Lord's death'.[1]

In Ignatius the line of attack of which these views form a part is directed unmistakably against the docetic heretics, who deny Jesus' true humanity and with it his birth too. Accordingly he stresses above all, and repeatedly, the 'carnal' reality of this event. With this the birth of Christ moves, as does the descent from David,[2] right over to the human side, with which the divine Being has indeed become united. But gazing in this direction tends to prevent in some degree the unfolding of the *miracle* of the birth as such. To Ignatius the humanity of the 'birth' is more important than the birth from the virgin. But in the framework of his theology it remains in the highest degree significant that the primary miracle of God's entry into the flesh and of his union with human nature is documented at this particular point by an obvious physical miracle, namely the virgin birth.

With all that, Ignatius bears the typical stamp of the whole of Greek theology and the corresponding way of understanding the virgin birth. The central place given to the incarnation, the monophysitic orientation of the Christology, and the anti-docetic emphasis on the virgin birth, which yet remains an indispensable miracle and '*mysterion*', will be repeated in essence and in the same sense by Irenaeus, by Athanasius, and by the later champions of the *Theotokos*. This certainly does not exclude a union with further themes and their progressive development. Ignatius with his understanding of the virgin birth is thus far a particularly 'pure' type that is still at the beginning.

In contrast there appears a generation later the next witness, *Justin*, as the similarly 'pure' representative of an apologetic treat-

[1] *Eph.* 19.1: καὶ ἔλαθεν τὸν ἄρχοντα τοῦ αἰῶνος τούτου ἡ παρθενία Μαρίας καὶ ὁ τοκετὸς αὐτῆς, ὁμοίως καὶ ὁ θάνατος τοῦ κυρίου· τρία μυστήρια κραυγῆς, ἅτινα ἐν ἡσυχίᾳ Θεοῦ ἐπράχθη. Certainly the preference for conception and birth in this passage is also brought home by the context. In *Magn.* 11 there appears instead the apter triad of birth, suffering, and resurrection (πεπληροφορῆσθαι ἐν τῇ γεννήσει καὶ τῷ πάθει καὶ τῇ ἀναστάσει τῇ γενομένη ἐν καιρῷ τῆς ἡγεμονίας Ποντίου Πιλάτου).

[2] According to this, Ignatius must have supposed Mary to have been a descendant of David; cf. *Eph.* 18.2: ὁ γὰρ Θεὸς ἡμῶν Ἰησοῦς ὁ Χριστὸς ἐκυοφορήθη ὑπὸ Μαρίας κατ᾽ οἰκονομίαν Θεοῦ ἐκ σπέρματος μὲν Δαυίδ, πνεύματος δὲ ἁγίου. Mary's descent from David is first expressly asserted by Justin, *Dial.* 45.4. He may have felt the difficulty of any written proof of this statement: Arthur Frhr. v. Ungern-Sternberg, *Der traditionelle alttestamentliche Schriftbeweis 'de Christo' und 'de evangelio' in der alten Kirche* (1913), 74.

ment of the virgin birth. For him, too, the Palestinian, Jesus' virgin birth is an established and undoubted piece of genuine Christian tradition. He himself hardly knows what theological line to take about it as a historical event;[1] but he feels all the more strongly the need to remove the obstacle that it may present to Christians, Jews, and pagans, and to ensure its position as a proved and established fact.[2] In this, no doubt, he already stands in a definite tradition that begins for us in Matthew's Gospel; but we can assume that in his thorough, zealous way he has gone far beyond his predecessors in this respect too. In any case the later defenders of the virgin birth have used his arguments again and again, and to that extent they have remained either directly or indirectly dependent on him.[3]

As has been said, Justin still knows Christians who regard Jesus as the son of Joseph and Mary.[4] He reproaches these people with a false trust in human dogmas.[5] No one who clings to God's word need on any account doubt the truth of the virgin birth. In this, however, Justin is thinking, not of the Gospels that he knows, but of the Old Testament prophecies, especially of the text from Isaiah[6] quoted by Matthew: 'Behold, a virgin shall conceive, and bear a son.'[7] It is nothing but hardness of heart if the Jews distrust the clear testimonies of the ancient Scriptures and will not accept the prophecy.[8] Justin refutes in detail their opinion that in the passage quoted not 'virgin' but 'young woman' is to be accepted as the correct translation,[9] and that the prophecy itself is to be applied

[1] It fits in with this that he hardly mentions the Spirit's part (strongly emphasized by Ignatius) in the conception of Jesus. It is mentioned once in *Apol.* I 33.5.

[2] Justin mentions the virgin birth innumerable times, but can also leave it unmentioned in asserting the incarnation: *Apol.* I 63.10; II 5(6).5; *Dial.* 125.

[3] Irenaeus will have obtained his material, as W. Bousset thinks (*Jüdisch-christlicher Schulbetrieb in Alexandria und Rom* [1915], 303), partly from one (?) source common to both; but, of course, he also used Justin himself.

[4] See p. 19 above.

[5] *Dial.* 48.4 (see p. 21, n. 2, above).

[6] Isa. 7.14, AV. The RSV has 'young woman' instead of 'virgin'.

[7] *Apol.* I 33; *Dial.* 43, 68, 84. For the corresponding exposition of the passion text of Isa. 53 cf. H. W. Wolff, *Jesaja 53 im Urchristentum* (1950), 131, 138; E. Fascher, *Jesaja 53 in christlicher und jüdischer Sicht* (1958), 23f.

[8] *Dial.* 44.

[9] On this dispute, in which the Ebionite Christian Symmachus is on the side of the Jews, see Schoeps, *Judenchristentum*, 73f., and *Aus frühchristlicher Zeit* (1950), 82ff.

not to Jesus Christ, but to the king of those days, Hezekiah.[1] But the promise of the virgin birth does not depend on this saying alone. For Justin the whole of the Old Testament is full of miraculous references and oracles relating to the story of Christ. Thus for example according to Justin, Jacob's blessing in Gen. 49 on Judah, Jesus' ancestor, who is to wash his garments in the blood of grapes, is a clear announcement of the virgin birth. For this passage testifies, not only—against all docetism—that Jesus really had 'blood' in his veins and was therefore a real human being, but also that this blood originated not through human seed, but—like the 'blood of grapes' —from 'God's strength', and therefore from the Holy Spirit. And this evidence, known also to Irenaeus,[2] which we feel to be so far-fetched, is regarded by Justin as so convincing that he not only repeats it several times against the Jews, but also produces it again for pagan readers as a particularly striking piece of evidence.[3]

But apart from this, Justin has a further argument to hand: it is even less possible for them to avoid believing in the virgin birth, as in fact their own mythology prefers to treat heroes and extra-ordinary personalities as sons of the gods, descended from Zeus.[4] As Justin knows quite well, this is a slightly dangerous argument from comparative 'religion' which the Jews like to bring in on the other side to defame the Christian birth story as pagan.[5] Of course, in Mary's case it is out of the question that some infatuated god had carnal intercourse with an earthly virgin; and as Justin empha-sizes, such ideas are not to be entertained for a moment.[6] At the same time he feels quite safe about this 'conjunction' of his case, and he knows that, if it is rightly understood, it can only result in renewed confirmation of the truth about Christ. For the pagan 'parallels' are not really genuine independent parallels at all, but in their turn only distorted reflections of the Christian message. The demons, being enemies of God, have long ago obtained through the

---

[1] *Dial.* 68, 71, 77, 84.

[2] *Demonstr.* 57 (53); see on this L. M. Froidevaux on his translation in SC 62 (1959), 120, n. 2.

[3] *Apol.* I 32.9–11; *Dial.* 54; 63.2; 76.2.

[4] *Apol.* I 21f.; 23.2f.; 54f.; *Dial.* 69f.; 78.6. In the environment of that time this idea could also be understood 'symbolically'; cf. A. D. Nock, *Conversion* (1933), 232ff.

[5] Tertullian, *Adv. Marc.* IV 10 (Kroymann, CSEL 47 [1906], p. 446) later manages to turn the same suspicion against Marcion's docetism.

[6] See especially *Apol.* I 33.3.

Old Testament prophets a certain knowledge of Jesus' future coming, on the strength of which they have themselves spread abroad in the world the lies about the supposed sons of the gods. They hoped that when the real Son of God appeared his value would be assessed accordingly and that no one would believe in him.[1]

As to the Jew, Justin can remind him that with God nothing is impossible, and that Christ's birth from the virgin would after all be no more unlikely than the creation of Eve from Adam's rib, or of all things that came directly through God's words.[2] Justin knows nothing of pagan nature stories, the examples of supposed partheno-genesis among bees, vultures, the phoenix, and so on, which will be brought in by later fathers. We do, however, find that he uses side by side almost all the rational possibilities of defending the virgin birth. Throughout they are apologetic arguments, which Justin, however strongly convinced he is of their fairness, brings himself to use only in actual defence against pagan or Jewish disbelief. For himself it is enough that, as he likes to remind the Jewish *Christians*, the virgin birth represents a biblical truth which as such allows of no doubt from the very first. Thus he makes positive use of it only within the context of his great Christological scriptural proof: the virgin birth is a particularly obvious instance of fulfilled prediction. That means that the concordant voice of biblical prophecy, on whose account Christ is to be believed, is authenticated in a particularly striking way by the virgin birth, which for its part supports the burden of scriptural proof, on which Justin's whole biblical theology intentionally concentrates. The inversion of the idea, according to which the miracle of the virgin birth could in its turn be made credible by the miracle of prophecy fulfilled,[3] is not yet put forward by Justin.[4] In spite of the formalistic rationalism and the wearisome prolixity with which he develops the truth and meaning of the virgin birth, Justin keeps entirely to the course begun by Matthew.

[1] *Dial.* 67, 69f.
[2] *Dial.* 84; cf. Tertullian, *Iud.* 13; *De carn. Chr.* 16.
[3] I find this argument first in Lactantius, *Inst.* IV 12:'. . . . quod sane incredibile posset uideri, nisi hoc futurum ante multa saecula prophetae cecinissent.'
[4] In the *Epistula apostolorum* 21 (32) the virgin birth becomes in its turn an argument for the credibility even of the resurrection.

The two streams of the apologetic and the dogmatic points of view meet at the end of the century in *Irenaeus*.[1] As is well known, Irenaeus is also characterized by his efforts to gather together the most diverse early traditions, and by combining them to achieve the broad basis of a 'Church' theology that will overcome the heresies.[2] For him, of course, the virgin birth is already a part of the old 'apostolic' tradition; Irenaeus upholds the rightness of the canon of the four Gospels.[3] But the Old Testament prophecies are more important to him all along than the birth stories in Matthew and Luke,[4] for by these prophecies the virgin birth is made a 'sign' against Jews and heretics which they cannot overlook.[5] This means that Irenaeus is here following Justin, whose polemic against the supposedly wrong translation of the Isaiah text he continues with an apologetic purpose.[6] Christ, it is now argued, would as Joseph's son not only be less than David or Solomon, but would not even have been entitled to an inheritance; for Jeconiah's posterity was expressly excluded by the prophet Jeremiah[7] from sovereignty.[8] Thus far the whole messiahship of Jesus depends on his virgin birth. Now, however, there is brought forward in addition to these considerations, very strongly and movingly, the real, essential meaning of the event. The Holy Spirit characterized through the words of the prophets on the one hand the actual birth that took place from the Virgin, and on the other hand Christ's inner being, derived from God.[9] In the rejection of docetism on the subject of the virgin birth, the actual birth is again stressed above everything,[10]

---

[1] The following were not available to me: J. Carçon, *La mariologie de S. Irénée* (Lyons, 1932), and B. Przybylski, *De mariologia S. Irenaei Lugdunensis* (Rome, 1937).

[2] Martin Widmann is very much to the point on this characteristic: 'Irenäus und seine theologischen Väter', *ZTK* 54 (1957), 156–73.

[3] See p. 21 above.

[4] But the agreement of the Isaianic prophecy with the apostles' testimony (= Matt. 1) is now expressly emphasized: *Haer.* III 21.4.

[5] τὸ τῆς παρθένου σημεῖον: *Haer.* III 21.1; cf. 20.3; 21.6.

[6] *Haer.* III 21.4f., introduced by the detailed account of the origin of the LXX: 21.3.

[7] Jer. 22.24f.

[8] *Haer.* III 21.9. For the historical background of this legitimacy problem in Judaism cf. K. Baltzer, *Das Ende des Staates Juda und die Messias-Frage* in *Studien zur Theologie der alttestamentl. Überlieferungen* (1961), 33–43.

[9] *Haer.* III 21.4.

[10] On this cf. especially A. Houssiau, *La christologie de S. Irénée* (Louvain and Gembloux, 1955), 236f. The emphasis on the carnal-earthly relationship connects

for on that depends the kinship with David and the membership of the race of Adam; the origin from the Spirit, on the other hand, makes Christ the Son of God; and it is only the union of the two sides that is the means of our redemption. 'For the Logos became man, and the Son of God the Son of man, so that man, who united with the Logos, should receive affiliation and become God's Son. Or how else should man unite with God, if God had not united with man?'[1] Irenaeus, too, moves along the lines of an essentially incarnational theology, and although he can quite well develop its meaning in this way even without regard to the virgin birth, a good deal of light can be thrown on it from this angle. Thus the virgin birth is given more weight than it would have as a mere 'sign'.

Meanwhile Irenaeus has progressed beyond the Lucan and Ignatian view in that he now also fixes his gaze on the virgin birth as such, and seeks to establish more precisely the objective necessity of the occurrence. This is carried out within the framework of the well-known concept of recapitulation, according to which Christ renews fallen and corrupt mankind in his own person and, following a great plan of salvation, takes up afresh and now carries to its conclusion the development that was begun in paradise and came to grief through Adam. Christ restores man's paradisal communion with God more richly and more fully in a new phase of the *Heilsgeschichte*. The development of this thought is carried out through the idea of the correspondence of type and antitype.[2] This means that the conditions and the events of the primal history have to be repeated in the life of Christ, in order that their old, fatal sequence may be overridden and replaced by one that terminates in salvation. This way of thought and its corresponding schematism were not invented by Irenaeus, but he carried them to their fullest development. Behind them there stands ultimately the ancient mythological

---

Irenaeus with Ignatius and Tertullian, and distinguishes him from the later fathers, who take the virgin birth above all as a sign of Christ's divinity: Wingren, *Man and the Incarnation*, 96; see p. 24, n. 1, above.

[1] *Haer*. IV 33.4.
[2] On this see Jean Daniélou, *Sacramentum futuri — études sur les origines de la typologie biblique* (Paris, 1950), Livre I, ch. III: 'Adam et le Christ chez Saint Irénée' (21-44).

idea of a return of first things in the last days, the ancient correspondence of the beginning of time and the end of time.[1]

In Jewish speculations on the last days it was already bound up with concern about the *Heilsgeschichte*, and here primitive Christianity had followed in its new Christological understanding of the connection with the end of history.[2] Paul in particular had emphatically applied to Christ the idea of a 'spiritual' Adam as opposed to the first, carnal Adam, and thus portrayed the universality and the superiority of the new Christian salvation.[3] The significance of this correspondence now extends its reach still further—it becomes a means of bringing the Old and the New 'Testament' firmly together, and of proving, against the Marcionites and other gnostic heretics, the coinherence of Christian redemption with the creation. Irenaeus therefore strives (with the help of older authorities) to show the existence of this correspondence point by point, and to prove that it is true according to Scripture. Through this the abundant points of agreement, which by Justin were made to serve almost exclusively as proof of prophecy, now take on as it were a life of their own.[4] The ideas of correspondence and recapitulation are more than a merely formal method of scriptural proof; they show that it is rooted in a general metaphysical cosmic law of the *Heilsgeschichte*—a law which causes us to recognize or presume that God's actions have meaning and purpose. To a modern mind Irenaeus' way of arguing in all this gets on to side-tracks and in part takes on an almost trifling aspect; but in spite of this the depth and greatness of the conception on which it is based is not to be mistaken. As a matter of fact, the struggle with the dualistic and antinomian lines of gnostic thought was not finally decided intellectually from this direction.

[1] We need not discuss here whether or how far this idea is in its turn connected more generally with ancient ideas of cosmic cyclical recurrence.

[2] On the significance of this 'first Christian historical understanding', especially in Matthew's Gospel, cf. the remarks by E. Käsemann, 'Die Anfänge christlicher Theologie', *ZTK* 57 (1960, 162–85), 174 ff.

[3] On this see A. Gelin, 'La doctrine paulinienne du Nouvel Adam', *BSFEM* 13 (1955), 15–23; Egon Brandenburger, *Adam und Christus — exegetisch-religionsgeschichtliche Untersuchung zu Röm. 5.12–21* (1962); also J. Jervell, *Imago Dei* (1960), 240ff.

[4] This is carried so far that Irenaeus assumes in all seriousness that Adam must have sinned and died on a Friday, because redemption took place through Jesus' death on a Friday: *Haer.* V 23.2; cf. Koch, *Virgo Eva*, 18.

We pursue Irenaeus' arguments only in so far as they have a direct bearing on the significance of the virgin birth. Within the large area of the Adam-Christ speculation defined by Paul and continued by Irenaeus, this is not generally the case.[1] A clear connection with the virgin birth is obtained only where Irenaeus comes to speak of the way in which the first and the last Adam were created. Both were called into life by God, and for both of them God used a 'virgin' substance to form their bodies: 'Just as that first-created Adam had his bodily substance from the untilled and still virgin earth and was formed by the hand of God (for God had as yet sent no rain, and man had not yet tilled the ground) . . . so he who was himself the Word took up [the origin] of Adam again into himself, and in recapitulating Adam rightly accepted birth from Mary, who was then still a virgin.' This idea is put forward quite seriously: 'It the first Adam had had a man for his father and had been begotten by "natural" seed, then it could rightly be asserted of the second Adam that he had been begotten by Joseph.'[2] A direct divine creation as in the first Adam could indeed not be considered for Christ, for he was expressly to share our Adamite nature, so as now to bequeath to it life instead of death;[3] but the analogy was kept none the less. Thus the virgin birth makes manifest on the human side, beyond its general purport as a sign and miracle, a higher relationship pointing mysteriously to God's plan for the world's redemption.[4] Thereby it has become theologically significant. Irenaeus frequently used this typological proof in his work, and for centuries numerous theologians followed him in it.

If this consideration of the virgin birth leaves Mary wholly in the background, she begins to take a more prominent place as soon as

---

[1] Cf., e.g., III 23, where at the most 23.7 (semen praedestinatum . . . quod fuit partus Mariae) makes some such slight reference. On the other hand, the virgin birth is again clearly emphasized in *Haer.* V 1.3.

[2] *Haer.* III 21.10; et quemadmodum protoplastus ille Adam de rudi terra et adhuc uirgine — nondum enim pluerat deus et homo non erat operatus terram (Gen. 2.5) — habuit substantiam et plasmatus est manu dei, id est uerbo dei — omnia enim per ipsum facta sunt (John 1.3) et sumpsit dominus limum a terra et plasmauit hominem (Gen. 2.7) —, ita recapitulans in se Adam ipse uerbum existens ex Maria, quae adhuc erat uirgo, recte accipiebat generationem Adae recapitulans. Si igitur primus Adam habuit patrem hominem et ex semine uiri natus est, merito dicerent et secundum Adam ex Ioseph esse generatum.

[3] *Haer.* V 1.2f.; Houssiau, *op. cit.*, 239f.

[4] *Haer.* III 18.7; cf. 5.1; *Demonstr.* 32f.

Eve, as well as Adam, is brought into the matter.[1] In Paul's thought this never happened; but now there are set in contrast not only Adam and Christ, man and man, but also woman and woman, with Eve's disobedience and Mary's obedience in faith. The comparison can be developed still further. At the time of the fall, Eve too, like Mary, was a virgin, and she, too, had a destined future husband; and just as the one brought about death for herself and the whole human race, so the other became the cause of salvation for herself and all mankind. Eve was turned away from God by an (evil) 'angel'; Mary listened to the joyful angelic message and received God himself. Everywhere, therefore, there is the most exact correspondence as if reflected in a mirror. The disobedience of the one virgin was to be set right by the obedience of the other; Eve is taken into protection, as it were, by Mary; for the knot that held our fetters had to be loosened again in the way in which it was tied.[2] It

[1] But even then this is not always the case. Thus *Haer.* V 21.1, on Gal. 4.4, reads: 'neque enim iuste uictus fuisset inimicus, nisi ex muliere homo esset, qui uicit eum.' Here the birth from the Virgin is fundamentally a matter of in-difference. Christ is therefore now characterized as one 'born of woman', so that he—not Mary—can be brought into a typological contrast with Eve.

[2] *Haer.* III 22.4: 'consequenter autem et Maria uirgo oboediens inuenitur dicens: ecce ancilla tua, domine, fiat mihi secundum uerbum tuum (Luke 1.38). Eua uero inobaudiens; non obaudiuit enim, cum adhuc esset uirgo. quemad-modum illa uirum quidem habens Adam, uirgo tamen adhuc existens — erant enim utrique nudi in paradiso et non confundebantur (Gen. 2.25), quoniam paulo ante facti non intellectum habebant filiorum generationis; oportebat enim illos primo adolescere, dehinc sic multiplicari — inobaudiens facta et sibi et universo generi humano causa facta est mortis, sic et Maria habens praedesti-natum uirum et tamen uirgo obaudiens et sibi et universo generi humano causa facta est salutis. et propter hoc lex eam, quae desponsata erat uiro, licet uirgo sit adhuc, uxorem eius, qui desponsauerat, uocat, eam quae est a Maria in Euam recirculationem significans, quia non aliter, quod conligatum est, solueretur, nisi ipsae compagines alligationis reflectantur retrorsus, uti primae coniunctiones soluantur per secundas, secundae rursus liberent primas, et euenit primam quidem compaginem a secunda colligatione soluere, secundam uero colligationem primae solutionis habere locum. et propter hoc dominus dicebat primos quidem nouissimos futuros et nouissimos primos (Matt. 19.30; 20.16). et propheta autem hoc idem significat dicens: pro patribus nati sunt tibi filii (Ps. 44.17[EVV 45.16]). primogenitus enim mortuorum natus dominus et in sinum suum recipiens pristinos patres regenerauit eos in uitam dei ipse initium uiuentium factus, quoniam Adam initium morientium factus est. Propter hoc et Lucas initium generationis a domino inchoans in Adam retulit significans, quoniam non illi hunc, sed hic illos in euangelium uitae regenerauit. Sic autem et Eua ino-baudientiae nodus solutionem accepit per obaudientiam Mariae; quod enim alligauit uirgo Eua per incredulitatem, hoc uirgo Maria soluit per fidem.'

goes without saying that Irenaeus did not take Mary into account for her own sake in discussions such as these,[1] and had no wish to attribute to her anything like active participation in the work of redemption.[2] The whole range of ideas is orientated Christologically;[3] it is Mary's first-born who has alone compensated for the ancestor's guilt. At the same time the virgin birth story and Jesus' mother gain, on the strength of this idea of correspondence, a certain independent interest that they had not previously had— even though the concrete details of this typology may have been taken entirely from the New Testament, preferably from Luke's Gospel. It is interesting to follow out a little the background of this development in the realm of the history of ideas.

Irenaeus was for a long time regarded as the originator of the strange comparison of Christ's virgin birth from Mary with the creation of Adam from the 'virgin' substance of the untilled earth. Successful efforts had been made to collect pre-Christian Jewish

---

Haer. V 19.1: 'Manifeste itaque in sua proprie uenientem dominum et sua propria eum baiulante conditione, quae baiulatur ab ipso, et recapitulationem eius, quae in ligno fuit, inobaudientiae per eam, quae in ligno est, obaudientiam facientem et seductione illa soluta, qua seducta est mala illa, quae iam uiro destinata erat uirgo Eua, per ueritatem euangelisata est bene ab angelo iam sub uiro uirgo Maria, quemadmodum enim illa per angelicum sermonem seducta est, ut effugeret deum praeuaricata uerbum eius, ita et haec per angelicum sermonem euangelisata est, ut portaret deum obaudiens eius uerbo; et si ea inobaudiret deo, sed et haec suasa est obaudire deo, ut uirginis Euae uirgo Maria fieret aduocata; et quemadmodum adstrictum est morti genus humanum per uirginem, saluatur per uirginem — aequa lance disposita uirginalis inobaudientia per uirginalem obaudientiam, adhuc enim protoplasti peccatum per correptionem primogeniti emendationem accipiens et serpentis prudentia deuicta in columbae simplicitate, uinculis autem illis resolutis, per quae alligati eramus morti.' For Adam and Christ this point of view is again pressed in *Haer.* III 18.7.

[1] On the question of Mary's personal holiness cf. *Haer.* III 16.7, where Christ rejects her *intempestiua festinatio* in Cana. The text of John 2.4 is also repeatedly expounded in this sense later.

[2] The wording *Haer.* III 21.7 on the Lord's *aduentus* into this world 'non operante in eum Ioseph, sed sola Maria cooperante dispositioni (= τῇ οἰκονομίᾳ)' has, of course, nothing as yet to do with 'co-operation' in the modern theological sense.

[3] Cf. A. Benoît, *Saint Irénée — introduction à l'étude de sa théologie* (1960), 226f., 240. This also holds good for Gregory of Nyssa, who again in *hom. in Cant.* XIII (PG 44, 1052) takes up the picture of Mary as παράκλητος ('aduocata', *Haer.* V 19.1; *Demonstr.* 33), although he already knows invocations to Mary that still seem unthinkable in Irenaeus' circles.

parallels to this use of language;[1] but as at best they could take only Adam into account, and never Christ and his virgin birth, they did not lead far. Now the new Coptic gnostic sources of Nag-Hammadi have all at once taken us beyond this. In the *Gospel of Philip*, the Greek text of which is put in the second century, we find the following saying:[2] 'Adam originated from two virgins—from the Spirit and from the virgin earth. Therefore Christ was created from a virgin, so that he could make good the false step that had been taken in the beginning.' The idea of a female Holy Spirit points back to eastern Semitic presuppositions, and is met with elsewhere.[3] It must certainly not be assumed that the author of the *Gospel of Philip* was dependent on Irenaeus' arguments for the passage just quoted. The theory of the 'two virgins' to which Adam owed his birth suggests that this idea has a most fantastically speculative and perhaps also ascetic background,[4] which Irenaeus cuts out by giving the typology an anti-gnostic turn, limiting it to a biblical environment, and trying to interpret it only according to its Christological meaning.[5] We must therefore probably look for the

---

[1] I. Löw, 'Die Erde als jungfräuliche Mutter Adams', *ZNW* 11 (1910), 168; H. Vollmer, *ibid.* 3 (1909), 324; 9 (1910), 168; 11 (1912), 95, where further literature is mentioned. Behind it there then emerges the general archaic idea of 'soil and woman'; cf. M. Eliade, *Die Religionen und das Heilige* (1954), 291ff.

[2] Ed. W. C. Till (Patristische Texte und Studien 2, 1963), 43f.

[3] Cf., e.g., Saying 17 of the *Gospel of Philip* (Till, 17), and also the older work by Selma Hirsch, *Die Vorstellung von einem weiblichen Pneuma hagion* (Diss. theol. Berlin, 1926).

[4] We may think of the co-operation of the different aeons by which Christ is produced—especially in Valentinian speculation: Iren. *Haer.* 12.6; Tert. *Praescr.* 33; Hippol. *Ref.* VI 51 (Marcus); VII 26f. (Basilides); VIII 9 (docetists); similarly in the *Apocryphon of John* 49f. (Till, *Die gnostischen Schriften des koptischen Papyrus Berolinensis 8502* [TU 60, 1955], 139f.), the creation of Adam, the perfect man, by the seven archons of Jaldabaoth.

[5] On the other hand, there even appears once in the later *Gospel of Bartholomew*, beside Mary, who has 'brought to nought the transgression of Eve' (4.6), Peter as 'the likeness of Adam' (4.5) (translation by M. R. James in *The Apocryphal New Testament* [1924], 173). The typology of the 'virgin earth' can still frequently be found after Irenaeus. We find it in Tertullian (*De carn. Chr.* 16f.), Pseudo-Tertullian (*Adv. Iud.* 13), Firmicus Maternus (25.2), Methodius (*Symp.* III 4), Athanasius (*C. Ar.* II 7), Ephraem (*Evang. concord. expos.*, Moesinger, pp. 2of.; Assemani, *Op. Syr.* II 397a), Amphilochius (*Isaac*, Ficker, p. 304), Pseudo-Gregory Thaumaturgus (*Nativ. Chr.* 14), John Chrysostom (*Mutat. nomin.* 2; *Hom. in I Cor.* 7.4), Ambrose (*In ps.* I.35), Gregory of Elvira (Batiffol, *Tractatus Origenis* [1900], 209), Augustine (*Genes. c. Manich.* II 23, 37; *Ep.* 190.25), John Cassian (*Coll.* V 6, 3), and certainly often elsewhere.

original home of this idea in a more or less gnostic *milieu* of the kind reflected, on the whole, in the *Gospel of Philip*.

The same thing may hold good for the second form of the direct parallelizing of Eve and Mary. Before Irenaeus it occurs once, in Justin's *Dialogue with Trypho*. Christ, we are told here in accordance with the scriptural evidence, has 'become man by the Virgin, in order that the disobedience which proceeded from the serpent might receive its destruction in the same manner from which it took its origin'.[1] Again we have type and antitype in contrast, here the obedience and there the disobedience of an intact virgin. The comparison has a more highly allegorical setting with Justin than with Irenaeus: the unspoilt virgin Eve 'received' the serpent's word, and as a result 'gave birth to' sin and death. It seems to me very unlikely that Irenaeus should have received solely from this one passage in Justin the stimulus to develop so broadly this contrast between Eve and Mary.[2] On the other hand, even in the writings of Justin himself the text stands in isolation. Justin always understands the Old Testament types merely in the sense of the prophetic sign, namely of prediction; and he does not entertain elsewhere the idea of an antitypical correspondence that is necessary in itself, as it is here; he is not familiar with it even for Christ and Adam.[3] It is therefore natural to assume that in this isolated passage he may out of deference to his scriptural evidence have taken his idea (otherwise

---

[1] *Dial.* 100.4f.: . . . . καὶ διὰ τῆς παρθένου ἄνθρωπος γεγονέναι, ἵνα καὶ δι᾽ ἧς ὁδοῦ ἡ ἀπὸ τοῦ ὄφεως παρακοὴ τὴν ἀρχὴν ἔλαβε, διὰ ταύτης τῆς ὁδοῦ καὶ κατάλυσιν λάβῃ. παρθένος γὰρ οὖσα Ἔυα καὶ ἄφθορος, τὸν λόγον τὸν ἀπὸ τοῦ ὄφεως συλλαβοῦσα, παρακοὴν καὶ θάνατον ἔτεκε· πίστιν δὲ καὶ χαρὰν λαβοῦσα Μαρία ἡ παρθένος, εὐαγγελιζομένου αὐτῇ Γαβριὴλ ἀγγέλου ὅτι πνεῦμα κυρίου ἐπ᾽ αὐτὴν ἐπελεύσεται καὶ δύναμις ὑψίστου ἐπισκιάσει αὐτήν, διὸ καὶ τὸ γεννώμενον ἐξ αὐτῆς ἅγιόν ἐστιν υἱὸς Θεοῦ, ἀπεκρίνατο· Γένοιτό μοι κατὰ τὸ ῥῆμά σου.

[2] Similarly G. Jouassard, 'Nouvelle Ève chez les pères anténicéens', *BSFEM* 12 (1954, 35–54), 51: 'Saint Irenaeus for his part may depend on many precursors, and not only on Justin, for this topic of Mary/Eve.'

[3] This, of course, is connected with the fact that Justin disregarded Paul and possibly felt that the speculation about Adam was gnostic. The slight comparison between Christ and Adam in connection with the story of the temptation, *Dial.* 103, is without importance; one need only compare it with Irenaeus, *Haer.* V 21.2. There is interest in the new kind of stress laid on this parallel in Apollinarius of Laodicea, *frag.* 10 on Matt. 4.11 (J. Reuss, *Matthäuskommentare aus der griechischen Kirche* [TU 61, 1957], 4):᾽ Ἀπολλινάριος ὁ παράφρων τροφάς φησιν ἐκ παραδείσου διηκόνουν αὐτῷ, ἵνα, ὥσπερ ὁ μὴ ἀποσχόμενος, οὗ προσετέτακτο, ᾽Αδὰμ τὴν ἐκεῖ τροφὴν ἀπωλώλήκει, οὕτως ὁ νέος ᾽Αδὰμ καὶ ὢν μὴ προσετάχθη, ἀποσχόμενος καθ᾽ ὑπερβολὴν ἀρετῆς εἰς τὸ ἐξ ἀρχῆς καλὸν ἀποκαταστῇ.

perhaps somewhat open to suspicion) from a different kind of source or tradition.[1] Again, it may have lain in the same sphere from which Irenaeus borrowed the comparison with the virgin earth—that is, in the circles of older gnosticizing speculation.[2]

But however this may be, in any case the allegorical and typological comparison of the two virginities is the first form of a theological interpretation and elaboration of the virgin birth, which on this point breaks through the silence of the New Testament and pushes out further in a direction of its own. One may say that Irenaeus interpreted and 'christianized' on biblical grounds the elements of this speculation,[3] just as Paul had done to the Adam-myth that had been handed on to him. But it is clear that the simple and theologically unambiguous basic scheme relating anthropology and Christology is profoundly shaken when Eve is brought into it, and that if the Mary-typology were further extended, one might thus be easily misled into obscuring the unique position of Christ

---

[1] That he (or Irenaeus, as the case may be) adhered in this matter 'à la tradition la plus ancienne du Christianisme' and preserved 'l'écho de la tradition la plus antique', as Daniélou claims in *Sacramentum futuri*, 32ff., is in any case a highly problematical assumption, which in view of what we find in the New Testament is most unlikely. This kind of assertion made by J. Lebon, 'L'apostolicité de la doctrine de la médiation mariale', *Recherches de Théologie ancienne et médiévale* 2 (1930), 129–59, was rightly contested by Koch, *Virgo Eva*, p. 25, n. 2.

[2] The themes of the virgin Eve's 'conception' and 'child-bearing' perhaps hovered here in the well-known gnostic fashion midway between pure allegory and concrete hypostatizing. Thus in the *Apocryphon of John* 58 (Till, p. 157) the serpent, as Eve's seducer, teaches 'the begetting (σπορά) of lust (ἐπιθυμία), of defilement and ruin, for these are useful to him'. Later, however, it says that Jaldabaoth ravished 'the virgin (παρθένος) who was standing at Adam's side' and 'begot the first son, likewise (ὁμοίως) the second', namely the righteous Eloim and the unrighteous Jave. 'Those are they who in the generations (γενεά) of all men are called Cain and Abel to the present day. The conjugal (γάμος) cohabitation (συνουσία) originated through the first ἄρχων' (62f.; Till, pp. 166f.). According to Epiphanius, *Haer.* XL 5.3f., the Archontici similarly taught the Cainites, XXXVIII 2, 6f., and the Sethians, XXXIX 2, who, however, gave Cain and Abel a different origin. On the other hand, Tertullian, *De carn. Chr.* 17, speaks in this context, taking up again the Eve-Mary typology, only of the 'diabolus fratricida' whom 'Eua concepit in utero ex diaboli uerbo.' The rabbinical speculation about the seduction of Eve and the consequent birth of Cain is referred to by R. M. Grant, *Gnosticism and Early Christianity* (1959), 103f.

[3] On the speculations of Jewish Gnostics about Eve, cf. the summary account (by now needing a supplement) by W. Staerk, 'Eva-Maria — ein Beitrag zur Denk- und Sprechweise der altkirchlichen Christologie', *ZNW* 33 (1934), 97–104.

and opening the door to unstable speculations and mythologizing. The loosening of the historical connection and the bringing in of Christ's appearance on earth through some heavenly aeonian powers or other, taking shape in Mary, appealed in any case to gnosticizing sentiment. But we cannot say that Irenaeus succumbed to this danger, and the same is true of the fathers who took over his typological outlook—they kept throughout strictly within the framework of the biblical *Heilsgeschichte*. Mary remains the earthly mother of Jesus, and becomes in no sense a great super-historical figure; her religious significance is confined to her being the chosen mother of Jesus. In the early Church we look in vain[1] for a 'Mariological' exposition of the apocalyptic woman clothed in the sun, and in the same way the prophecy about the woman's seed, who is to bruise the serpent's head,[2] the so-called *protevangelium* of Genesis, is always related to Christ alone, and never to Mary.[3] Nor does the systematic amalgamation of Mary's person with the Church's reality take its origin in the orthodox section of the early Church.[4]

---

[1] This is shown with commendable clarity by P. Prigent, *Apocalypse 12 — Histoire de l'exégèse* (1959), which takes in the older literature as far as B. J. Le Frois, *The Woman clothed with the Sun (Rev. 12)—Individual or collective* (Rome, 1954), and A. Laurentin, 'L'interprétation de la Genèse 3.15 dans la tradition jusqu'au début du XIIIe siècle', *BSFEM* 12 (1954), 77–156. A. T. Kassing, *Die Kirche und Maria — Ihr Verhältnis im 12. Kap. der Apokalypse* (1958), goes to work more cautiously, but thinks that beside the ecclesiological interpretation of God's people, which results from the biblical-Jewish tradition, for the first half of the vision in Rev. 12.1–6 one can also discern a 'partly Marian sense'. Cf. by the same author: 'Der heilsgeschichtliche Ort Mariens in der Kirche nach Apk. 12' in *Maria et Ecclesia (Actus congressus Mariologico-Mariani, Lourdes 1958)* 3 (Rome, 1959), 39–60. In the case of a scholarly assessment such as that of F. Spedalieri, 'Maria et Ecclesia in Apocalypsi XII', *ibid.*, pp. 61–67, the conclusions are even more favourable.

[2] Gen. 3.15.

[3] Cf. F. Drevniak, *Die Mariologische Deutung von Gen. 3.15* (Diss. theol. kath. Breslau, 1934). The contrasting pseudo-learned presentations by J. Unger, *The First Gospel Gen. 3.15* (New York, 1954) and 'Mary is the Woman of the First Gospel (Gen. 3.15)', *Marianum* 18 (1956), 62–72, clearly indicate on the other hand a retrograde step in criticism. The same might be said of T. Gallus, *Interpretatio mariologica protevangelii*, etc. (Rome, 1949); cf. W. Delius, *Theologische Zeitschrift* 10 (1954), 452f., and J. C. De Moor, 'De Roomskatholieke Mariologie en de uitleg van Genesis III 15 bij Ephraem Syrus', *Gereformeerde Theologisch Tijdschrift* 59 (1959), 97–117.

[4] On occasion, of course, we come across references in connection with devotional-exegetical expositions, e.g. in Irenaeus, *Haer.* III 10.2; Tertullian, *De carne. Chr.* 7 (and see p. 48, n. 2) and *Adv. Marc.* II 4; Peter Chrysologus,

All attempts to spin out the patristic speculations in the opposite direction and thereby make them fruitful Mariologically merely show that that kind of thing remained quite unfamiliar to the early Church.[1] As far as we know, it was the Gnostics, and especially the Manichaeans, who first amalgamated the 'most chaste' virgin with the 'unspotted Church'[2] or with the 'heavenly Jerusalem' 'where the Lord went in and out', and so, in the words of an early medieval formula of abjuration, 'under the pretence of conferring honour insult Mary the holy Mother of God.'[3]

Thus the Mariological importance of the whole Eve-Mary typology in Irenaeus and his successors should not be overrated.

---

sermo 146; on Ambrose and Augustine see p. 78, n. 7, and p. 80, n. 4, below But these must not be artificially isolated and interpreted as unique 'Mariological' utterances; they are of no importance for a systematic inquiry. The whole area of the problem needs to be worked through thoroughly and critically; some materials, which are capable of being added to, are provided by Koch, *Virgo Eva*, 92–94, and Mich. Planque, art. 'Ève' in *Dictionnaire de Spiritualité* IV (1960, col. 1772–88) 1784–87.

[1] This is also true of the work by Alois Müller, written from a historical angle with ample material, *Ecclesia—Maria: Die Einheit Marias und der Kirche* (1955[2]), and even more for the scholastically constructive surveys, on the basis of the author's and other people's studies of the fathers; e.g. Stanislaus M. Llopart, 'Maria—Ecclesia. Observationes in argumentum iuxta patres praeephesinos' in *Maria et Ecclesia* 3 (see p. 43, n. 1), 81–107.

[2] *Acta Arch.* 55 (Beeson, GCS [1906], p. 81). We cannot well count this heretic, as does G. Söll, 'Maria-Kirche bei den griechischen Vätern seit Cyrill von Alexandrien' in *Maria et Ecclesia* 3 (137–62), 139, among the Church's 'witnesses' of the early years who offer 'a more or less clear identification of Mary and Church'; Epiphanius, *Haer.* LXXVIII 19, to whom he appeals, admittedly only 'intended' (?) this equalization; the supposed utterance of Cyril (*Hom. div.* 4), which apparently ratifies it, is not genuine: see p. 70, n.1 below.

[3] A. Adam, *Texte zum Manichäismus* (1954), 102. The formula comes from the ninth century. Herr Adam was kind enough to explain the text in question to me as follows: 'The noteworthy passage is not aimed primarily at the Paulicians, who were suspected in the ninth century as Manichaeans. It may be accepted as probable that the doctrine mentioned belonged to the Manichaean tradition. It is true that the person who often appears in the Psalter as "Blessed Mary" is probably Mary Magdalene; but in *Kephalaia* p. 94.4 Mary will have to be understood for "Eve". The idea of the great formula of abjuration seems to me to be related to the Valentinian view that Mary was only a "place of passage", a channel (Iren. *Haer.* I.2) for Christ. That the Manichaeans equate this "place of passage" with paradise probably goes back to Bardesanes: "A place of rapture are the gates that by virtue of (divine) ordinance are opened before the mother" (Patr. Syr. 12, Paris, 1907, p. 504); it is Ephraem who says that paradise means the mother's womb. The Manichaeans will not have been influenced by IV Esdras 10.44.'

To how small a degree Mary as a holy person forms the centre of interest can be realized from the fact that the comparison with Eve must by no means be concentrated on her alone. 'Generally speaking, every woman who plays a part in the salvation of God's people can be understood exegetically as a type of the new Eve'.[1] Even in Hippolytus, for example, the women who go to the grave on Easter morning are similarly contrasted with Eve[2]—a kind of view that lasts into the fifth century[3]—and Origen compares the two 'holy women', Elizabeth and Mary, with Eve.[4] Ambrose parallelizes

---

[1] Planque, 'Eve', col. 1779. As a temptress Eve has, of course, had other successors since the fourth century, e.g. Job's wife, or the high priest's maid who brought about Peter's denial: *ibid.*, col. 1772f.

[2] Hippol., *Cant.* XV on 3.1-4 (Bonwetsch, GCS I 1 [1897], 354f.): Christ meets them 'so that women too may become apostles, and make manifest the fault of the first Eve's disobedience by present rectifying obedience. . . . Eve becomes an apostle. . . . Eve a helper of Adam.' Daniélou, *Sacramentum futuri*, p. 36, n. 1, was the first to point out the tradition that begins here, but he did not yet recognize its general character (which Planque, *op. cit.*, col. 1785f., rightly emphasizes and illustrates) and therefore concentrates it one-sidedly on Mary Magdalene. Cf. further P. Joussard, *Nouvelle Ève*, pp. 42–45.

[3] Similar expositions about the 'sanctae mulieres' are to be found in Ambrose (*De Isaac* 43; *Exp. Lc.* X 156f.), Augustine (*Sermo* CCXXXII 2.2), Gregory of Nyssa (*C. Eunom.* III tom. 10.16f.), and Severus of Antioch (PO 16, 806ff.). In Ephraem (Moesinger, p. 270) Mary the mother appears herself at the grave—perhaps in connection with the Diatessaron (Bauer, *Leben Jesu*, p. 263); but such a tradition is widespread: C. Gianelli, 'Témoignages patristiques d'une apparition du Christ ressuscité à la vierge Marie', *Revue des études byzantines* 11 (Mélanges M. Jugie, 1933), 106–19; further references, especially to Gregory Palamas, in an article in Russian by Cypr. Kern, 'The appearances of the risen Lord to the Mother of God', *La pensée orthodoxe* 8 (1951), 86–112. There is interest in a further Ephraem text, which can hardly be genuine (Lamy I 531–3) which L. Hammersberger quotes in *Die Mariologie der ephremischen Schriften* (Diss. theol. Fribourg, 1938), 80. Here the risen Lord bids Mary Magdalene 'approach and see the resurrection of the Lord. But why did he first reveal his resurrection to a woman and not to men? There is revealed to us here a mystery regarding the Church and the mother of the Lord. The first knowledge of his arrival on earth was given to a virgin; his resurrection he himself revealed to a woman. At the beginning and at the end the name of the one who gave him birth is there and is made known. A Mary received him in the conception and saw the angel before her at his grave. . . .' Here we obviously have an attempt to bring Hippolytus' typology into line with the exclusive Eve-Mary typology. We find a similar passage, which is given a more marked allegorical turn, in Ambrose, *Virginit.* 4.20: 'tunc ait illi dominus: Maria (John 20.16) respice ad me. quando non credit, mulier est; quando conuerti incipit, Maria uocatur, h.e. nomen eius accipit, quae parturit Christum; est anima, quae spiritualiter parit Christum.' See below, p. 46, n. 1.

[4] *Hom. in. Lc.* VIII; in *Hom. in. Gen.* XII 3 they are Rebecca, Elizabeth, and Mary.

Eve and Sarah,[1] and emphasizes that there were many Marys before the one Mary brought the great fulfilment.[2] Christ, who as a man is said to have been born of a virgin, therefore does justice to both sexes in like manner. By the virgin birth Mary returns the thanks of the female sex for the rib received from Adam, from which she was formed,[3] and so on. Again and again it is a question here of the 'woman' or 'the women' as such, who thus receive their due.[4] Nothing like that would have been possible if the Eve-Mary typology had had only a 'Mariological' meaning from the outset. From our modern theological points of view we must not ask too much of the flexible methods of early Christian exegesis.

An ample summary of the various older ideas about the virgin birth is supplied once more, at the beginning of the third century, by *Tertullian*. Of course, he regards the virgin birth as a dogmatic necessity, even if he still has to defend it against 'Ebion', Marcion, and other heretics.[5] Christ has instituted a new beginning in the history of mankind, and the new, unique occurrence of a virgin birth corresponds to this *novitas* of his historical existence.[6] From the spiritual seed of Christ there was to proceed, according to the witness of the prophets, a new, spiritual mankind.[7] If the Son of God had had an earthly father as well as the heavenly Father, he would have had two fathers.[8] That is one of the rhetorically pointed

---

[1] Ambrose, *Inst. virg.* 5.32; *Ps.* CXVIII 22.30; on this B. Capelle, 'Le thème de la nouvelle Ève chez les anciens docteurs latins', *BSFEM* 12 (1954, 55–76), 57f. Further evidence in the comprehensive collection of Eve-Mary texts by H. Barré in 'Le "mystère" d'Ève à la fin de l'époque patristique en occident', *BSFEM* 13 (1955), 61–97.

[2] Ambrose, *Inst. virg.* 5.33f. It is only in Ambrose that the expositions have a more markedly 'Mariological' accent.

[3] Cyril of Jerusalem, *cat.* XII 29; cf. Pseudo-Hippolytus, *Theoph.* 7.

[4] See p. 38, n. 1 above on Irenaeus.

[5] Against the Ebionites: *Praescr.* 33; *Virg. vel.* 6.33; *De carne Chr.* 14, 16, 19, 24; Marcionites and Gnostics: *Praescr.* 33; *Valent.* 19f.; *De carne Chr.* 1; *Adv. Marc.* IV 10, Jews: *Spect.* 13; *Jud.* 9.

[6] *De carne. Chr.* 17 (Kroymann, 232): noue nasci debebat nouae natiuitatis dedicator. . . .

[7] *De carne Chr.* 17f.

[8] *Adv. Marc.* IV 10 (Kroymann, 446: 'ceterum duo iam patres habebuntur, deus et homo, si non uirgo sit mater. habebit enim uirum, ut uirgo non sit, et habendo uirum duos patres faciet, deum et hominem, et qui et dei et hominis esset filius'. On this cf. the *Gospel of Philip* 17 (Till, p. 17): 'And the Lord [would] not [have] said, "My [Father who art] in heaven" unless [he] had had (yet) a[nother] father; but he would simply have said, ["My Father"].'

turns of speech beloved of Tertullian,[1] the kind of saying often coined in such a way expressly for the virgin birth.[2] Its striking precision gives a false suggestion of logical necessity to which it has no claim. The typological comparisons, too, play their part again with Tertullian—he appeals both to the 'virgin' earth[3] and to the corresponding status of Eve and Mary,[4] and explains the scriptural evidence for the virgin birth in terms of the predicted sign and of the unique sublimity of the Lord.[5]

But it is where he sets out the virgin birth again especially as a birth, and as a proof, against gnosticism, of Jesus' true natural humanity, that Tertullian brings his greatest weight to bear and develops real theological ardour.[6] In this he follows the same polemical line that we have already observed in Ignatius, and which is also uppermost in the period that followed him. But Tertullian certainly goes further than all his predecessors and successors in his hatred of docetic spiritualism and the way in which, in gnosticism, reality tends to evaporate. He not only stresses the 'folly' of the actual birth of a god, and the virgin birth as the furthest limit of that folly,[7] but he also, in his crass realism, sometimes borders on the barely tolerable. He takes the unaesthetic features of an

[1] A similarly striking contrast can be achieved with the physical and spiritual 'seed', *De carne Chr.* 17 (Kroymann, 232): 'haec est natiuitas noua, dum homo nascitur in deo, ex quo in homine natus est deus, carne antiqui seminis suscepta sine semine antiquo, ut illam nouo semine id est spiritali reformaret exclusis antiquitatis sordibus expiatum'; on this W. Bender, *Die Lehre über den Heiligen Geist bei Tertullian* (1961), 74f.

[2] Cf. e.g., Lactantius, *Inst.* IV 25: 'habebat enim spiritalem patrem deum, et sicut pater spiritus eius deus sine matre, ita mater corporis eius uirgo sine patre'. The same thought is developed more amply by Augustine, *Sermo* 140.2. In Pseudo-Athanasius, *Incarn, c. Ar.* 8 (PG 26, 996A), we read: αὐτὸς οὖν μητέρα ἔχει μόνον ἐπὶ γῆς καὶ ἡμεῖς πατέρα μόνον ἔχομεν ἐν οὐρανῷ. Similarly John Chrysostom, *Hom. Heb. de Melchis.*, (PG 56, 259f.); *Prophet. obscur.* 1 (*ibid.*, 166f.); Gregory of Nazianzus, *Or. theol.* III 19 (PG 36, 1000): ἀπάτωρ ἐντεῦθεν, ἀλλὰ καὶ ἀμήτωρ ἐκεῖθεν, and similarly Ambrose, *Myst.* 46, and Augustine, *Joh. ev. tr.* II 15.

[3] See p. 40, n. 5, above.

[4] *De carne Chr.* 17.

[5] In this the quotation from Isa. 7 again plays the main part; e.g. *Jud.* 9; *De carne Chr.* 17; *Adv. Marc.* IV 10. The reference to pagan mythology now loses its positive sense as a 'connection', and becomes essentially polemical: *Apol.* 21.7ff.; *Marc.* IV 10.

[6] The arguments that Justin, *Dial.* 75 (Otto 270) had brought forward for the *virgin* birth change in Tertullian simply into arguments for the *birth*: *De carne Chr.* 3.

[7] *De carne Chr.* 4; *Iud.* 9.

actual human birth and rearing, and describes them in all their medical details with repellent plainness,[1] so as to make known unmistakably the full significance and the paradoxical truth of a god who really became man—not without the corresponding pitiable suffering of the Redeemer on the cross.

Tertullian is not in any way interested in anything that goes beyond the biblical text in glorifying Mary's human person and sanctity.[2] There is in his writings no suspicion of any ascetic elucidation of the 'virgin' and of Mary's later marriage, which, in fact, Irenaeus, too, thinks of as an actual marriage that was physically consummated.[3] He holds firmly to the biblical tradition, which he regards as incontestable, according to which it was only up to the birth of Jesus, the first-born, that Joseph abstained from marital intercourse, and that Jesus had brothers.[4] In all his practical ecclesiastical writings, so very amply developed, Tertullian only once uses the idea of Christ's virgin birth with a 'moral' implication—

---

[1] *Adv. Marc.* IV 21; *De carne Chr.* 4.20, 23.

[2] Martha and Mary stand closer to Jesus than his mother; the latter is once described in contrast to the Church as an image of the unbelieving synagogue, *De carne Chr.* 7 (Kroymann, 210ff.): 'fratres domini non crediderunt in illum . . . mater aeque non demonstratur adhaesisse illi, cum Martha at Maria aliaeque in commercio eius frequententur . . . figura est synagogae in matre abiuncta et Iudaeorum in fratribus incredulis. foris erat in illis Israel, discipuli autem noui intus audientes et credentes cohaerentes Christo ecclesiam deliniabant, quam potiorem matrem et digniorem fraternitatem recusato carnali genere nuncupauit'; in conformity with this, Augustine, *Enarr. ps.* 127.12. Tertullian develops the exposition in such detail because the relevant text, Matt. 12.48, as a supposed denial of his mother by Jesus himself, provided a main support for those Gnostics who contested his birth, *Adv. Marc.* IV 19 (Kroymann, 482): 'uenimus ad constantissimum argumentum omnium, qui domini natiuitatem in controuersiam deferunt: ipse, inquiunt, contestatur se non esse natum dicendo: quae mihi mater et qui mihi fratres?'

[3] Hugo Koch, *Adhuc virgo* (1929), 8–13; *Virgo Eva* (1937), 17–60.

[4] Cf., e.g., *Monog.* 8; *De carne Chr.* 7, and against the Gnostic invention of a *uiriginitas in partu* the classic definition of the 'uirgo quantum a uiro, non uirgo quantum a partu', *De carne Chr.* 23. On the whole area of the problem the reader may be referred here to H. Koch, *Adhuc virgo*, 3–7, and *Virgo Eva*, 8–17. Attempts to discredit his expositions of Irenaeus and Tertullian need no refutation; they refute themselves. I am of the opinion that Koch still sees Irenaeus and Tertullian, who is alleged to depend on him, too much in isolation. In the West before Hilary—that is, up to the middle of the fourth century—there is no witness at all for the 'semper virgo'; and that can hardly be a mere chance: see pp. 72 f. below. Hippolytus, too, regards the 'brothers of Jesus' as the children of Joseph and Mary; cf. L. Mariès, *Hippolyte de Rome, Sur les bénédictions d'Isaac, de Jacob et de Moïse* (PO 27.1 [1954], 150f.: ' "Ses frères" a-t-il dit (Deut. 33.9): Ceux qui, selon la chair, étaient considérés comme étant ses

and even there it is not really a matter of 'virginity', but of rejecting vice. Today, he says in connection with a theological discussion of repentance, there is no longer any excuse for unchastity, after Christ has descended into human flesh that was not even opened to the custom of marriage, in order then not even to marry (legitimately),[1] but rather to go forward instead to the cross of suffering. The whole declamation, with its rhetorical conclusion *a minore ad maius*, shows once more how far from the opponent of gnosticism any ascetic interpretation of the virgin birth in itself necessarily lay— and in this he agrees not only with the older fathers, but also with Scriptures, which he marshals, not without effect, so indefatigably in all his theses.

In later years, as the gnostic danger gradually dies away, the treatment of the virgin birth becomes perceptibly less prominent. It seems to me that this has not hitherto been taken sufficiently into account.[2] The typological pattern, rare even with Tertullian, is hardly used any longer in the third century,[3] and the references to

---

frères, ceux-là, le Sauveur ne les a pas reconnus, parce qu'ils n'étaient pas véritablement frères. Certains étaient nés de la semence de Joseph, mais Lui, d'une vierge et du Saint Esprit' = N. Bonwetsch, 'Hippolyts Erklärung der Segnungen des Moses' 10 (in TU 26, 1a [1904], p. 59) (one of the few early witnesses of importance whom Koch has overlooked): 'He did [not] acknowledge as brothers those who were regarded as his brothers according to the body; the Redeemer did not acknowledge them, because in truth those [were] not his brothers who were born from Joseph through seed, but he from the Virgin and the Holy Spirit; and they regarded them as his brothers, but he did not acknowledge them.' In any case, I cannot agree with Koch when he says (*Virgo Eva*, 64) that Tertullian was 'the first to take over a perpetual virginity of the Lord's mother if it met him anywhere definitely and authoritatively'. That does not yet, in fact, seem to have been the case within the Great Church; but he would never, for intrinsic reasons, have accepted such 'witnesses' as are offered by the *Protevangelium of James* or the *Ascension of Isaiah* (and see p. 54, n. 2 below), even if he had not detected their 'historical' inadequacy.

[1] A similar connecting of Christ's 'virginity' with his virgin birth appears too in *De carne Chr.* 20 (Kroymann, 241): '. . . uti uirgo est et regeneratio nostra spiritaliter ab omnibus inquinamentis sanctificata per Christum uirginem et ipsum etiam carnaliter ut ex uirginis carne.'

[2] But I. Ortiz de Urbina has already observed, 'Lo sviluppo della mariologia nella Patrologia Orientale', *Orientalia Christiana Periodica* 6 (1940, 40–82), 50: 'After the period of the eastern apologists we enter a phase in which very little attention is paid to the problem of Mariology.'

[3] It is entirely absent in Clement of Alexandria, Hippolytus, and also Origen. There is at most a modest exception here in the (authentic?) fr. 21 on Luke 1.28 (Rauer, GCS IX² [1959], 235): (*a*) Ἐπειδὴ εἶπεν ὁ Θεὸς τῇ Εὕᾳ «ἐν λύπαις τέξῃ

Mary are correspondingly rare. When the typological comparison with Eve begins again in the fourth century, especially in sermons, and undergoes a frequently devotionally poetic development,[1] it has lost its earlier theological importance, which it will not recover, in a changed interpretation, till the Middle Ages. The learned theologian *Julius Africanus* notices the difference between the Matthean and the Lucan genealogical trees of Jesus, and is the first to suggest as a way out—with which he himself is not fully satisfied —that we may distinguish between a natural and a legal parentage, Luke having (partly) followed the latter, and Matthew the former.[2] But as regards the question of the virgin birth such considerations remain unessential. The theology of the Alexandrian School has rightly from 'Mariological' standpoints been called 'wretched'.[3] It is just as completely misleading when one tries to honour, shall we say, *Hippolytus* as a great 'Mariologist'.[4] With him the Eve-Mary typology has quite disappeared.[5] Of course, he, too, in his anti-

---

τέκνα», διὰ τοῦτο λέγει ὁ ἄγγελος· «χαῖρε κεχαριτομένη.» αὕτη γὰρ ἡ χαρὰ λύει ἐκείνην τὴν λύπην· (b) εἰ γὰρ διὰ τὴν τῆς Εὔας κατάραν διέβη ἡ ἀρὰ ἐπὶ πᾶν τὸ τῶν θηλειῶν γένος, οὐκοῦν στοχαστέον, ὅτι διὰ τῆς πρὸς τὴν Μαρίαν εὐλογίας πλατύνεται ἡ χαρὰ ἐπὶ πᾶσαν ψυχὴν παρθένον.
Methodius is familiar with the comparison of the Virgin with the virgin earth (*Symp.* III 4) and the Adam-Christ typology (*Symp.* III 4f., 8), but not with the connecting of Eve with Mary. This latter is also true of Eusebius of Caesarea; cf. especially *C. Marcell.* II 1.

[1] I am not pursuing this development any further; but from the point of view of the art and tradition of rhetorical preaching it would be fascinating in itself to do so; cf. meanwhile Jouassard (see above, p. 41, n. 2) and T. Camelot, 'Marie, la nouvelle Ève dans la patristique grecque du concile de Nicée à saint Jean Damascène', *BSFEM* 12 (1954), 157–72; A. Wenger, 'La nouvelle Ève dans la théologie byzantine', *ibid.*, 13 (1955), 43–60.
[2] His letter to Aristides discussing this question is taken from Eusebius, *HE* I 7: M. J. Routh, *Reliquiae sacrae* (1946²) 231ff., 334ff.
[3] O. Stegmüller, art. 'Alexandrinische Schule' in *LMK* I 1, 127.
[4] This claim has been made by Hugo Rahner even by the attribution of an unauthentic fragment 'Hippolyt von Rom als Zeuge für den Ausdruck Θεοτόκος', *Zeitschrift für katholische Theologie.* 59 (1935), 73–81. But this is quite out of the question: L. Mariès, PO 27 (1954), VIIf.; S. Lyonnet, 'Contribution récente des littératures armènienne et géorgienne à l'exégèse biblique', I, *Biblica* 39 (1958), 488f.
[5] This is all the more worthy of notice as his Adam-Christ typology brings in the virgin birth: *Dan.* IV 11; *Deut. fr.* 1;*Noet.* 17 (Schwartz, *Zwei Predigten Hippolyts* [1936], 16. 31ff.). In these circumstances we can expect no special Mariological allusion even in the obscure passage of the (in my opinion undoubtedly) Hippolytan ending in the *Epistle to Diognetus* 12.8; on the text cf.

heretical writings opposes the docetist and Jewish denial of the virgin birth,[1] and in this he now also appeals expressly to the Church's confession of faith.[2] He repeatedly describes Jesus as having been miraculously born of the holy Virgin;[3] but there he remains entirely on the traditional lines, without achieving any theological progress. His own interests go in the other direction, concentrating more than hitherto on questions of the passion instead of on the incarnation. Even the argument from the 'blood of grapes'[4] is now no longer a prophecy of the virgin birth, but of the Lord's sufferings.[5]

This Mariologically indifferent attitude is at that time specially typical of the West. In the works of *Cyprian* and *Novatian* Mary is mentioned only two or three times by each—and then only in passing —especially in conjunction with scriptural evidence,[6] in Novatian still with the usual anti-docetic emphasis.[7] Cyprian's disregard of Mary[8] is particularly striking because he himself was not only an ascetic, but, especially in the writings for 'virgins', also a zealous champion of ascetic ideals.[9] But it is never Mary who appears as the example in this sense, but always Christ alone, and he only in

---

further H. I. Marrou, *A Diognète* (SC 1951), 83, n. 6; 239, n. 1; Jouassard, *Nouvelle Ève*, 49.—On the typological relation between Eve and the women at the grave of Christ, see pp. 44 f. above.

[1] *Ref.* V 26; VII 33f., 35; *Noet.* 3 (Schwartz, 6.28f.).
[2] Cf. F. Kattenbusch, *Das apostolische Symbol* 2 (1900), 354ff.
[3] Cf., e.g. *Dan.* IV 39; *Antichr.* 4.28; *Deut.* 33.1; *Ps. fr.* 19, 25. Nearly all the passages echo confessional formulae. In Ps. fr. 18 there is a contrasting of Jesus' human and divine qualities in connection with the angelic annunciation, the shepherds' adoration, Simeon, Anna, the magi and their star, and the wedding at Cana—but the virgin birth does not appear at all.
[4] See p. 32.
[5] *Antichr.* 11; *Bened. Mosis* 18; *Pentat. fr.* 17; otherwise *Gen. fr.* 24. Tertullian, too, is familiar with the reference to the passion and the eucharist: *Adv. Marc.* IV 40. Cf. further M. Simonetti, 'Note su antichi commenti alle Benedizioni dei Patriarchi', *Ann. Fac. di Lettere-Filosofia e Magistero* 28 (1960), 1–71, and 'Osservazioni sul De benedictionibus patriarcharum di Rufino di Aquileia', *Rivista di cultura classica e medioevale* 4 (1962), 3–44.
[6] Cyprian: *Test.* III 73 (relevant quotations also in III 75f.); Novatian: *Trin.* 28, both times with reference to Isa. 7.
[7] *Trin.* 24.
[8] Besides the quotations mentioned in n. 6 above, the only other mentions of Mary in his writings, also in quasi-credal phrases, are in *Idol.* 11; *Ep.* 72.5.
[9] Cf. Koch, *Virgo Eva*, 72f.

isolation, as he himself lived 'immaculately', not through any appeal to his virgin birth.[1] A new development of our problem is not native to the Latin West; on the contrary, it begins, as does all theological life, in the eastern part of the ancient civilized world, the real cradle of Christianity.

[1] *Habit. virg.* 3, 5, 7.

III

The Virgin Birth
Under the Influence of Ascetic Thought

IN THE struggle against gnosticism the appraisement of the virgin birth had been essentially 'dogmatic'. As a birth, it established the true humanity of Jesus Christ, and beyond that its typological interpretation emphasized the positive place that had been given to the One who had miraculously become flesh, in relation to the creation and the whole of the ancient *Heilsgeschichte*. Alongside that, a moral interpretation of the event was not in practice taken into account. Any such interpretation could, indeed, only have been ascetic;[1] and the ascetic leanings of Gnostics and other radical sectarians excluded as a matter of course any explanation of that kind. But, on the other hand, early Christianity had from the outset not been unfamiliar with leanings towards asceticism.[2] Since the end of the second century these had also been pushing their way up with increased energy within the 'catholic' Church. In this spirit we find, first in the East, a new approach to the primitive witness, less at first in pure theology than in popular piety. The virgin birth in its sanctity works as a counterpart of natural sexual activity; and Mary, the virgin mother, then appears as the prototype of purity and chastity, and the object of admiration. It will certainly be a long time before such sentiments have penetrated theology and entirely absorbed or pushed aside the opposing elements of the older tradition. Nor must their importance for the simple piety of the community be overestimated, or generalized too quickly with arguments from the comparative study of religions or the psychology of religion; but there does actually begin here something decisively new that points to the future.

[1] On an exception of this kind in Tertullian, see pp. 47f. above.
[2] H. von Campenhausen, 'Die Askese im Urchristentum' in *Tradition und Leben* (1960), 114ff.

The earliest connected document that we have demonstrating the new way of regarding the matter is an apocryphal Greek book about Mary's early years—the book now called the *Protevangelium of James*.[1] It claims to have been written by James, the Lord's brother. The account extends from the promise of Mary's birth to the birth of Jesus, and even for a period beyond that. The groundwork of the writing might be put in the middle, or at the latest at the end, of the second century. For the *Protevangelium of James* on the one hand takes for granted the great canonical Gospels, but on the other hand it amplifies and corrects them with an ingenuousness that would hardly have been possible at a later time, even in heretical circles. In general, it has no polemical theological impress at all. The narrator wishes particularly to glorify Mary's miraculous life, and to describe her as the unsullied image of ascetic perfection. Thus we hear of her miraculous origin—the theme of the childless parents to whom a child is promised and given in their old age is once again repeated—and of her saintly childhood and upbringing in the temple, till she is entrusted to the aged widower Joseph, who, of course, has no idea at all of making 'the virgin of the Lord' his actual wife. The miraculous continuance of her virginity, even after the birth of Christ, is accordingly extolled in a fantastic way: Salome, who doubts whether Mary is physically inviolate, has her investigating hand consumed as if by fire, and restored only through a miracle by the Christ child. That the holy mother remains a virgin all her life is a matter of course. Jesus' brothers, about whom the older evangelists' accounts had agreed, are summarily turned into stepbrothers from Joseph's first marriage. Unfortunately it cannot be determined more precisely where this writing comes from. The only thing that seems certain is that it cannot have originated in Jewish Christian circles; nor, however, can it be asserted that it was subjected, in its fantasy and asceticism, to 'gnostic' or any other heretical 'influence'.[2]

[1] Edition by M. Testuz, *Papyrus Bodmer V—Nativité de Marie* (Cologny-Geneva, 1958); on the orientation O. Cullmann in Hennecke and Schneemelcher, *NT Apocrypha* I, 370ff.

[2] The same is true of the Inscription of Abercius, which probably means Christ when it refers, 13f., to the ἰχθὺν ἀπὸ πηγῆς, ὃν ἐδράξατο παρθένος ἁγνή; on the exposition cf. T. Klauser, art. 'Abercius' in *RAC* I, 15f. The explanation of the 'holy virgin' is not so certain: both Mary and the Church (though hardly both at the same time) could be meant. In the first case the inscription would be

The first Church father who seems to have been familiar with this apocryphon is *Clement of Alexandria*. Although he is no stranger to the older points of view in the treatment of the virgin birth,[1] he shows in his own way, when he mentions it, a far-reaching indifference towards the historical tradition as such; he at once makes it the subject of purely allegorical reflections. One feels the connection with the exegetical tradition of gnosticism. Clement certainly speaks of the Church as a virgin mother, and particularizes this motherhood in varied allegory;[2] but in this context it is not Mary who is being discussed. Instead, she appears once as the type of the eternally virgin Scripture. The allegory is so developed that Mary is not regarded as the mother of a newly born child, and this— so Clement observes—has actually been asserted of her by some witnesses.[3] It is clear from the context that Clement has his eye on

---

'one of the oldest documents of the faith of the first Christians in the virginal conception': S. Grill, *LMK* I 1, 22f. On the other hand, the gnostic imprint of the *Odes of Solomon*, which also come from the second century, is indisputable. Here, 19.7, the miraculous painless birth without a midwife is mentioned. Still more fantastic is the description in the *Ascension of Isaiah* 11.7–14; cf. the translation of the text (handed down in various languages) by R. H. Charles (1900), 76f.: 'And after two months of days while Joseph was in his house, and Mary his wife, but both alone, it came to pass, that when they were alone, that straightway Mary looked with her eyes and saw a small babe, and she was astonied. And after she had been astonied, her womb was found as formerly before she had conceived. And when her husband Joseph said unto her, "What has astonied thee?" his eyes were opened, and he saw the infant and praised God, because into his portion God had come. And a voice came to them: "Tell this vision to no one." And the story regarding the infant was noised abroad in Bethlehem. Some said, "The Virgin Mary hath born a child, before she was married two months." And many said, "She has not borne a child, nor has the midwife gone up (to her), nor have we heard the cries of (labour) pains." And they were all blinded respecting Him, and they all knew regarding Him, though they knew not whence He was.'

[1] Thus he discusses the genealogical tree, *Strom.* I 147.5, and refers, *Strom.* VI 127.1, to the prophetic announcement of the virgin birth.
[2] *Paed.* I 41.3–42.2. It is a question here of an extremely complicated and moreover, a badly transmitted text, whose ideas remind one of the Inscription of Abercius (see p. 54, n. 2 above); for the elucidation cf. W. Völker, *Der wahre Gnostiker nach Clemens Alexandrinus* (1952), 154, 156.
[3] *Strom.* VII 93.7–94.2: 'Ἀλλ', ὡς ἔοικεν, τοῖς πολλοῖς καὶ μέχρι νῦν δοκεῖ ἡ Μαριὰμ λεχὼ εἶναι διὰ τὴν τοῦ παιδίου γέννησιν, οὐκ οὖσα λεχώ (καὶ γὰρ μετὰ τὸ τεκεῖν αὐτὴν μαιωθεῖσάν φασί τινες παρθένον εὑρεθῆναι). τοιαῦται δ' ἡμῖν αἱ κυριακαὶ γραφαί, τὴν ἀλήθειαν ἀποτίκτουσαι καὶ μένουσαι παρθένοι μετὰ τῆς ἐπικρύψεως τῶν τῆς ἀληθείας μυστηρίων. «τέτοκεν καὶ οὐ τέτοκεν», φησίν ἡ γραφή, ὡς ἂν ἐξ αὐτῆς, οὐκ ἐκ συνδυασμοῦ συλλαβοῦσα.

the *Protevangelium* tradition, but does not want to discuss further the question of its possible trustworthiness.[1] For all that, it seems that he is himself following the theory according to which Jesus' brothers were stepbrothers from Joseph's first marriage.[2] In this matter Clement, whose attitude to marriage was by no means hostile,[3] may have been prompted less by an ascetic line of thought than by a general feeling of taste and the aesthetic consideration that also plays a part elsewhere in this question. Not all natures are carved out of such hard wood as Tertullian, and as soon as one begins to think out Mary's later marriage on the supposition of the previous virgin birth, there automatically appears a certain resistance,[4] to which the dogmatic construction can then accommodate itself.

It is a different matter with an older contemporary of Clement, the author of the treatise on the resurrection ascribed to Justin.[5] This certainly goes back to the second century, and its author is the

---

[1] Very much to the point here is Karl Rahner, 'Virginitas in Partu' in J. Betz and H. Fries, *Kirche und Überlieferung* (Geiselmann-Festschrift, 1960, pp. 52–80), 66f. = *Schriften zur Theologie* 4 (1960, pp. 173–205), 189f. I cannot find, however, that, as G. Söll, 'Die Anfänge mariologischer Tradition' (*ibid.*, pp. 35–51), 47, thinks, Clement makes use of this tradition only 'with some uneasiness'.

[2] *Adumbr. in. ep. Jud.* 1 (Stählin, GCS III [1909], p. 206). That Hegesippus (Eusebius, *HE* III 20.1) had already formed this judgment cannot be proved from the traditional text: Koch, *Virgo Eva*, 88, n. 2.

[3] In *Strom.* III 102 he even infers—against the Gnostics—from the Lord's virgin birth, that birth in general cannot be anything bad. On the other hand Origen, *Hom. Lev.* VIII 3, says that the pious have rightly cursed their birth; on this cf. H. Karpp, *Probleme altchristlicher Anthropologie* (1950), 197, n. 1. According to I Tim. 2.15 it is only the θεία τεκνογονία that has brought honour to Mary's τεκνογονία and to the whole female sex: *Hom. Luc. fr.* 32c (Rauer, p. 239).

[4] Cf. Koch, *Virgo Eva*, 85f., and lately, e.g., E. Stauffer, 'Petrus und Jakobus in Jerusalem', in Roesle and Cullmann, *Begegnung der Christen* (1959, pp. 361–72) 367f., n. 46.

[5] According to W. Delius, 'Pseudo-Justin "Über die Auferstehung",' *Theologia Viatorum* 4 (1953), 181–204, it was Melito of Sardis; this agrees with an early hypothesis of A. Harnack, *Die Überlieferung der griechischen Apologeten* (1882) 163, n. 147 (cf. *Geschichte der altchristlichen Literatur* II 1 [1958²], 510). The ascetic temper would fit in well with the theology of the 'eunuch' (Eusebius, *HE* V 24.5), who may possibly for that very reason have been suspect to the later Church; cf. C. Andresen, art. 'Melito' in *RGG IV*, 846. But Andresen himself, as he informs me by letter, because of the theological differences from the newly discovered Paschal Homily, does not regard Melito as the author of the 'Pseudo-Justin' treatise. In this Paschal Homily (Lohse 10.39; 11.30) and in the other fragments of Melito (cf. Koch, *Virgo Eva*, pp. 64f.) only quasi-credal references to the virgin birth are met with.

first Christian theologian whose judgment of the virgin birth is determined by a radically ascetic sentiment, and who consequently maintains that, strictly speaking, it was a necessity. 'Our Lord Jesus Christ was born of a virgin only for the following reason: he was to bring to naught the begetting that proceeds from lawless appetite, and provide the ruler of this world with the proof that God could form man even without human sexual intercourse.'[1] It is therefore supposed that even a begetting in wedlock implies something common, profligate, and indeed in opposition to God's will and 'law', something whose conquest Christ even in his earthly origin demonstrates to the devil. This, the text proceeds, is then confirmed by the further course of his life. Those things that the flesh needs if man is to live—food, drink, and clothing—Christ has taken for his use (and thus far rejected the *gnosis* that is fundamentally hostile to the world); but sexual activity is by no means necessary to man; and therefore Christ did not practise it, but presented in his life the pattern of a pure, immaculate mode of conduct. No doubt the demand for, or the ideal of, 'celibacy for all baptized people'[2] would be in line with such ideas; but, of course, the Church could not in any case at that particular time, in the anti-gnostic and anti-Montanistic struggle, accept any such radical asceticism. Thus the interpretation of the virgin birth set out here shows no results for the time being. Nevertheless the lines of thought that can be traced in connection with it continue their influence; they form the most important presupposition for the new interest in the sanctity of Mary's person and for a corresponding understanding of Jesus' virgin birth.

It is important to determine correctly the position taken up by *Origen* in this connection. He was the first to bring the ascetic themes in the framework of catholic ecclesiastical thought into relation with Mary's person (with pseudo-Justin that had not yet been the case), and to develop them, to a certain degree, independently. At the same time Origen was not, as he is sometimes supposed to

---

[1] K. Holl, *Fragmente vornicänischer Kirchenväter in den Sacra Parallela* (1899), 39: καὶ ὁ κύριος δὲ ἡμῶν Ἰησοῦς ὁ Χριστὸς οὐ δι' ἄλλο τι ἐκ παρθένου ἐγεννήθη, ἀλλ' ἵνα καταργήσῃ γέννησιν ἐπιθυμίας ἀνόμου καὶ δείξῃ τῷ ἄρχοντι καὶ δίχα συνουσίας ἀνθρωπίνης δυνατὴν εἶναι τῷ Θεῷ τὴν ἀνθρώπου πλάσιν. . . .

[2] Karl Müller, *Die Ehelosigkeit für alle Getauften in der alten Kirche* (1927; = *Aus der akademischen Arbeit* [1930], 63ff.); see further H. Chadwick, art. 'Enkratiten', *RAC* V, 351ff.

have been, an enthusiastic champion of Marian devotion. We must take care to see his relevant utterances in right proportion.[1] In the whole of his theological reflections and the immense quantity of his writings, the occasional remarks about Mary are not central to his argument, and have no special importance. But what Origen says is always well thought out and deserves to be taken seriously, even when it is only a matter of practical and edifying considerations for the community.

We see the significance of his work even in the apologetic expositions of the virgin birth. Here Origen is neither original nor creative; but all the arguments that his predecessors have marshalled he takes up again, puts carefully in order, develops, and in part continues and supplements with fresh thoughts.[2] Thus, as far as we know, Origen was the first theologian to ponder deeply the question why Christ had to be born of a virgin engaged to be married.[3] He answers that it was possible only in that way to protect her from the suspicion of adultery, and that moreover in that way the Saviour's birth was concealed from the devil—a matter on which he appeals to Ignatius.[4] (Later theologians have expanded Origen's suggestion by considerably increasing the number of reasons.)[5] Besides that, Origen, of course, revives Justin's prophetic evidence[6]

[1] A convenient summary of the relevant texts in a 'Corpus Mariologicum' is provided by D. Cipriano Vagaggini, '*Maria nelle opere di Origene*' (OCA 131, 1942), 177–220, though with a somewhat one-sided preference for the Latin tradition.

[2] Vagaggini writes appropriately, *op. cit.*, 68: '. . . by the time of Origen the polemic against the Jews and pagans on the subject of Mary's virginal conception has almost ceased. Not that his writings contain no references to it; quite the contrary; but he is induced to treat the subject mainly with a view to providing a methodical refutation of the *Alethes Logos* of the philosopher Celsus.'

[3] *Hom. Luc.* VI (Rauer, 34f.).

[4] *Eph.* 19.1 (see p. 30, n. 1 above).

[5] So Theodore of Heraclea, *fr.* 4 on Matt. 1.24 in J. Reuss, *Matthäuskommentare aus der griechischen Kirche* (TU 61, 1957), 57; Ambrose, *Exp. Luc.* II 1; *Instit. virg.* 6.42; Jerome, *Comm. Matt.* 1.18; cf. T. Zahn, *Forschungen zur Geschichte des NT Kanons* 2 (1883), 32f., n.

[6] Here he has to go afresh, *C. Cels.* I 34, into the question of the translation of Isa. 7.14 (see p. 31 above). Not that later theologians have found it any more possible to avoid doing so; but while Origen in his conscientiousness strives first for a philological parallel (Antonie Wlosok, 'Nichtcyprianische Bibelzitate bei Laktanz', *Studia Patristica* IV [TU 79, 1961, pp. 234–50], 240, n. 4), they often content themselves with baldly insulting the Jewish translators as unbelieving liars; thus, e.g., Cyril of Jerusalem, *Cat.* XII 2, 21. This *catechesis* is, moreover, an interesting piece of evidence that the prophetic proof, whose apologetic

and defends the possibility of the miracle of the birth in the same way with reference to the omnipotence of God, the first creation, the mythological parallels, and now the supposed examples of parthenogenesis in nature.[1] It is declared positively that for the fulfilment of his calling Jesus had on the one hand to be united to human beings and possess something in common with them, and therefore come in the body from Mary's human flesh; and that on the other hand he ought also to show some quality beyond the ordinary, so that his soul could remain untouched by all evil.[2] But this rather uninspired motive for the virgin birth does not stand in the centre of the argument, which concentrates primarily on the Jewish reproach, taken up again by Celsus, that Jesus was the offspring of adultery. According to Origen that is an impossibility, if only because 'according to experience' none but inferior people are produced by illicit unions, whereas Jesus' personality was of unique moral elevation and purity. The nature, and therefore the origin, of body and soul must correspond to each other.[3] We see how the typically Origenistic blurring of theological and anthropological lines of thought can also accommodate contemporary biological ideas.[4]

---

importance in respect of Jews and pagans has receded in the victorious Church of the empire, still remains essential in respect of catechumens (*Cat.* XII 5, 16).

[1] *C. Cels.* I 37; in addition the example of the worm, *Hom. Luc.* XIV (Rauer, p. 91).
[2] *C. Cels.* I 33: διὰ τί οὐχὶ καὶ ψυχή τις ἔσται πάντῃ παράδοξον ἀναλαμβάνουσα σῶμα, ἔχον μέν τι κοινὸν πρὸς τοὺς ἀνθρώπους, ἵνα καὶ συνδιατρίψαι αὐτοῖς δυνηθῇ, ἔχον δέ τι καὶ ἐξαίρετον, ἵνα τῆς κακιᾶς ἀγευστος ἡ ψυχὴ διαμεῖναι δυνηθῇ; cf. *Comm. Joh.* I 31 (34). 220 (Preuschen, GCS IV [1903], p.39); *Hom. Luc.* VII (Rauer, p. 45).
[3] *C. Cels.* I 32f.
[4] *Comm. ser. Matt.* 50 (Klostermann, GCS XI [1933], p. 109); Jesus' physical advantages, too, seem to be associated with his virgin birth: 'non solum autem exaltauit eum secundum spiritum, sed etiam secundum corpus (ut per omnia sit exaltatus), et corpus, quod suscepit de uirtute altissimi et de uirgine huiusmodi ministerium ministrante'; cf. Karpp, *Anthropologie*, 196f. From this angle there is some interest in the strange argument that Methodius, *Res.* I 26, ascribes to his Origenist who denies the resurrection of the flesh: one might appeal against this to Christ's bodily resurrection, ἀλλὰ τὸ Χριστοῦ σῶμα οὐκ ἦν ἐκ θελήματος ἀνδρός (John 1.13), ἡδονῆς ὕπνῳ συνελθούσης (Wisd. 7.2), ἀλλὰ ἐκ πνεύματος ἁγίου καὶ δυνάμεως ὑψίστου (Luke 1.35) καὶ παρθένου, τὸ δὲ σὸν ὕπνος ἐστὶ καὶ ἡδονὴ καὶ ῥύπος. Christ therefore gained, through his birth which did not proceed from human sensuousness, a bodily nature of a different kind, and could therefore, in contrast to all other men, be resurrected in the body.

In exegetical contexts Origen sometimes, of course, has occasion to speak about Mary. Although his exposition is sometimes very wide, it does not for the most part go more deeply into the biographical relationships, but in general passes quickly over into the symbolic and allegorical. In this connection Mary is scarcely preferred to other biblical figures.[1] The exposition of the Song of Solomon is still in no way orientated 'Mariologically', nor does the title 'bride' appear as yet for Mary.[2] Similarly Origen is far from thinking of crediting Mary with personal sinlessness. Joseph and Mary—the sequence is characteristic[3]—have been obliged in the course of Jesus' life to go through a development in their faith and in their understanding of salvation. In this respect the exposition of Simeon's prophecy[4] is specially characteristic; this has been repeated times without number[5]—sometimes with qualifications—in the writings of the later Greek fathers[6] and is again echoed in John of Damascus.[7] The 'sword' that is to pierce Mary's soul de-

[1] See p. 45 above. Her typicality is stressed by way of example, *Comm. Joh.* I 4 (6). 23; *Hom. Gen.* XII 3.

[2] K. Wittenkemper, art. 'Braut' in *LMK* I 5, 898ff. The gnostic antecedents of the idea (cf., e.g., Hippolytus, *Ref.* VI 34.4) are not taken into account here, while on the other hand J. Schmid, art. 'Brautschaft, heilige' in *RAC* II, 528–64, does not go at all into Mary's relationship to Christ. It seems to me certain that the title 'bride' was first used to denote ascetic 'virgins' and from here onwards was transferred to Mary. Its previous stage is not to be sought in the relationship between Christ and the Church (Christ and Eve, Christ and Mary). As regards Mary the findings are still completely negative for the third century, though allegorical exegesis may by chance lead on occasion to an apparent approach to the bride-idea, as with Hippolytus, *Antichr.* 4 (Achelis, GCS I 2 [1897], 6). In the fourth century the examples in the Greek fathers are still extremely scanty. There once appears clearly, in Cyril of Jerusalem, *Cat.* XII 26, the designation of Mary as τῆς παρθένου τῆς ἀγίας νύμφης. On the other hand, the title 'bride' plays a large part in Ephraem; cf., e.g., *De nativ.* 16.10: 'For I am Thy sister, of the house of David the father of us Both. Again, I am Thy Mother because of Thy sanctification, Thy handmaid and Thy daughter, from the Blood and Water wherewith Thou hast purchased me and baptized me' (translation, Nicene and Post-Nicene Fathers XI, 245).

[3] In Vagaggini's paraphrases it is regularly reversed. In fact, in *Hom. Luc.* XIX (Rauer, p. 116), in rejecting a wrong judgment about Mary and Joseph, reads: 'amoue hanc opinionem *maxime* a Joseph. . . .'

[4] Thus on Luke 2.41ff., *Hom. Luc.* XX (Rauer, p. 121): 'et quia necdum plenam fidem Joseph et Maria habebant, propterea sursum cum eo permanere non poterant, sed dicitur descendisse cum eis'; on this cf. Vagaggini, *op. cit.*, 157–62.

[5] Luke 2.35.

[6] Cf. the list of authors specified by Vagaggini, *op. cit.*, p. 206.

[7] *De fide orthod.* IV 14, § 91; cf. *Sacra parall.* Δ 26; on this the rather timid

notes, according to this, the doubt by which even she must be
overtaken at the sight of the passion. But we cannot assume, says
Origen, that she alone was immune from being 'offended' at that
time, when even the apostles and Peter himself were 'offended'
because of Jesus.[1] If Mary had then been exempt from all temptation, Christ would not have died for her sins; for 'all have sinned'
and need redemption through him.[2]

All this is no longer noticeable in the framework of the early
Church's theology. On the other hand, the detailed critical reflections now beginning about Mary's perpetual virginity are important.
In the spirit of his life's ascetic ideal Origen answered this question
personally in a more definitely affirmative way than Clement; but
the biblical foundation causes him difficulties. Obviously in his
time and *milieu* the wish is often expressed for such a portrait of
Mary;[3] but it is not yet as simple to ignore the statements in the
opposite sense in Matthew's and Luke's Gospels as was done by
later theologians whose belief in the '*aeiparthenia*' had become a
matter of course—as far as and including Luther. Characteristic of
this is the standpoint of an unnamed 'heretic' who still clings to the
biblical idea of Mary's wedlock and tries from this to explain
Jesus' supposed denial of his mother: Jesus, he says, renounced
Mary—it is obviously a question of an interpretation of Matt.
12.48[4]—because he was indignant that after his miraculous birth

---

remarks with which V. Grumel, 'La mariologie de Saint Jean Damascène',
Echos d'Orient 40 (1937, 318–46), 328ff., rejects the arbitrary fresh interpretation
of C. Chevalier, *La mariologie de Saint Jean Damascène* (*OCA* 109, 1936).

[1] On this order of rank cf. the competition in modesty in the *Gospel of Bartholomew* 2.4 (*Apocryphal New Testament*, tr. M. R. James, 170ff.), but which
here at last ends in Mary's favour.

[2] *Hom. Luc.* XVII (Rauer, p. 106): 'ergo scandalizati sunt universi in tantum,
ut Petrus quoque, apostolorum princeps, tertio denegarit, quid putamus, quod
scandalizatis apostolis mater domini a scandalo fuerit immunis? si scandalum
in domini passione non passa est, non est mortuus Iesus pro peccatis eius. si
autem omnes peccauerunt et indigent gloria dei, iustificati gratia eius et redempti
(Rom. 3.23), utique et Maria illo tempore scandalizata est'; on this cf. Vagaggini,
162–8. The Greek text is preserved only in fragments; the reference to Peter and
the apostles is no longer covered by it.

[3] This is the case, for instance, in the Christian interpolations of the *Oracula
Sibyllina*: J. B. Bauer, 'Die Messiasmutter in den *Oracula Sibyllina*', *Marianum*
18 (1956), 118–24.

[4] The interpretation of this text has always caused difficulties, from Christological as well as from 'Mariological' points of view. The Gnostics tried on this

she had been conjugally united with Joseph and had conceived further children.[1] In the face of such reflections it would, of course, have been the simplest thing possible for Mary's ascetic defenders to appeal at once to the *Protevangelium of James* or similar productions, and, as Origen knows, 'some' actually did so.[2] But although Origen himself feels no repugnance to the ascetic bias of this literature,[3] he knows that it is open to objections, and therefore disdains to rely on its evidence.[4] So there is nothing else for him to do than to begin with the tortuous interpretations reminiscent of Rabbula to which from now on the New Testament texts have to conform: Jesus' 'alleged' brothers, he explains, are indeed not produced expressly as Mary's sons; but on the other hand it is not at all necessary to take the Bible in its most obvious sense where it describes Jesus as 'first-born' and says that Joseph abstains from conjugal intercourse 'until' the birth took place.[5] Jesus' brothers were his stepbrothers, and Joseph and Mary never came to full conjugal intercourse.[6]

---

basis to deny altogether Jesus' human origin: Tertullian, *Adv. Marc.* IV 19 (see p. 48, n. 2, above); Epiphanius, *Haer.* XXX 14.5. Titus of Bostra says on the same text, 'The messenger of Mary and the brothers may have discharged his commission in an unmannerly way and mocked Jesus' humble origin': J. Sickenberger, *Titus von Bostra—Studien zu dessen Lukashomilien* (TU 21.1, 1901), 105, n. 1.

[1] *Hom. Luc.* VII (Rauer, 43): . . . . ὅτι ἐτολμησέ τις εἰπεῖν κατὰ τῆς Μαρίας, ὡς ἄρα ὁ σωτὴρ αὐτὴν ἠρνήσατο, ἐπεί, φησίν, συνήφθη μετὰ τὴν ἀπότεξιν τὴν τοῦ σωτῆρος τῷ 'Ιωσήφ; on this cf. Vagaggini, *op. cit.*, 130–4.

[2] *Comm. Matt.* X 17 (Klostermann, 21): τοὺς δὲ ἀδελφοὺς 'Ιησοῦ φασί τινες εἶναι, ἐκ παραδόσεως ὁρμώμενοι τοῦ ἐπιγεγραμμένου κατὰ Πέτρον εὐαγγελίου ἢ τῆς βίβλου 'Ιακώβου, υἱοὺς 'Ιωσὴφ ἐκ προτέρας γυναικὸς συνῳκηκυίας αὐτῷ πρὸ τῆς Μαρίας. οἱ δὲ ταῦτα λέγοντες τὸ ἀξίωμα τῆς Μαρίας ἐν παρθενίᾳ τηρεῖν μέχρι τέλους βούλονται . . . .

[3] Thus he reports in *Comm. Matt. ser.* 25 an apocryphal παράδοσις, in consequence of which Zechariah was murdered by the Jews because he had acknowledged Mary's virginity; cf. H. v. Campenhausen, 'Das Martyrium des Zacharias', *Historisches Jahrbuch* 77 (1958), 383ff.

[4] A. v. Harnack, *Der kirchengeschichtliche Ertrag der exegetischen Arbeiten des Origenes* 2 (1919), 37.

[5] *Hom. Luc.* VII (Rauer, 44): 'porro quod asserunt eam nupsisse post partum, unde approbent, non habent; hi enim filii, qui Ioseph dicebantur, non erant orti de Maria, neque est ulla scriptura, quae ista commemoret.' Cf. also the subtle explanation of John 19.26 in *Comm.* I 4.23.

[6] *Comm. Joh. fr.* 31 on 2.11 (Preuschen, 506f.). But Origen does not yet concern himself—*pace* Vagaggini (*op. cit.*, 88)—with the problem of a *virginitas in partu*: Koch, *Virgo Eva*, 68ff.

In connection with such theses Origen does once speak out for Mary as the given pattern of ascetic women. After the Holy Spirit has come over her and the power from on high has overshadowed her, it is impossible for Mary to have shared her bed with a man. 'I think, therefore, that Jesus was the first fruits of holy purity for men, but Mary for women; for it would not sound fitting if one would single out anyone instead of her as the first fruits of virginity.'[1] This assertion represents something new. It would not be right, however, to ascribe any special importance to an isolated remark of that kind. It had no perceptible results; on the contrary, even after Origen, Mary plays a noticeably small part in the ascetic literature of the third and even the fourth century.[2] Even *Methodius*, with all his excessive praise of virginity, makes virtually no use of Mary as a symbol.[3] The same is true, indeed, of *Athanasius*,[4] and,

---

[1] *Comm. Matt.* X 17 (Klostermann, 21f.): καὶ οἶμαι λόγον ἔχειν, ἀνδρῶν μὲν καθαρότητος τῆς ἐν ἁγνείᾳ ἀπαρχὴν γεγονέναι τὸν Ἰησοῦν, γυναικῶν δὲ τὴν Μαρίαν· οὐ γὰρ εὔφημον, ἄλλη παρ' ἐκείνην τὴν ἀπαρχὴν τῆς παρθενίας ἐπιγράψασθαι.

[2] The sermons of Gregory Thaumaturgus on the annunciation are known not to be genuine: Ch. Martin, 'Note sur deux homélies attribuées à saint Grégoire le Thaumaturge', *Revue d'historie ecclésiastique* 24 (1928), 364–73. Eusebius of Caesarea has no independent interest at all in Mary. He hardly mentions the 'Virgin' except in phrases which echo the formulae of the confession of faith (*Dem. ev.* II 3, 150f.; IV 10; VII 1, 15) and of the traditional scriptural evidence (*Dem. ev.* III 2.51; VII 1.30, 36, 85), and in discussing the text of Luke 1.30ff. (*Dem. ev.* VII 1.97f.). In *Vit. Const.* III 43 she is called θεοτόκος. Cf. p. 49, n. 3, above.

[3] Only once, in the great closing hymn of the *Symposium*, is the Virgin mentioned last of all beside other examples of virginity—Abel, Joseph, Jephthah's daughter, Judith, and Susanna: *Symp.* XI 290. Otherwise Christ is always in the centre, and is also the very archetype of ἁγνεία. Further references to the Virgin are in the main reminiscent of formulae and are without interest as in *Sanguis.* 7.5; 10.3. If the Old Slavic text is reliable, she is already described, 8.2, as 'holy'. Apparently the name 'Mary' does not occur in Methodius at all.

[4] For the dogmatic writings and the *Vita Antonii* the findings are clear. Athanasius extols virginity as the truly Christian way of virtue, and traces it back again and again to Christ: *Incarn.* 51; *Apol. ad Const.* 33; *Vita Ant.* 91, 94; *Ep. ad Amun.* etc. Further, according to G. Söll, art. 'Athanasios', *LMK* I 3/4, 388, he is 'not really a Mariologist, but a resolute champion of the Christological and soteriological foundations of Mary's status as Mother of God and as a virgin'. His whole theology has a strictly Christological outlook, and Mary has absolutely no independent significance in it. In line with this, the virgin birth is not only explained on the traditional anti-docetic lines (*Incarn.* 8, 20; *Ad Epict.* 5), but is now emphatically asserted, in opposition to the Arians, to be a sign of Christ's true divinity—e.g. *Incarn.* 18, 49; *Ad Epict.* 11; *Ad Maxim.* 2; *C. Arian.* III 31. The traditional scriptural evidence, too, is now turned in this direction: *Incarn.* 33–40. See p. 24, n. 1, above, and p. 70 below.

as far as I can see, of all the great theologians of the fourth century.[1] *Gregory* of Nazianzus begins, in the style of the new veneration of saints, to heap up particularly on Mary, 'the Mother of God', the eulogies that emphasize her purity and holiness.[2] But this hardly changes the total picture and dogmatic position of her person. Mary's sinlessness presents as yet no problem anywhere in Greek theology. But when John *Chrysostom*, who in many respects stands on the opposite wing to Gregory, misses no opportunity in his sermons of drawing attention expressly to Mary's human shortcomings and weaknesses, we can hardly interpret this surprising attitude otherwise than by supposing that he sees dangers approaching from that quarter and is consciously trying to take a stand against his community's inclinations towards the glorification of Mary.[3]

The only 'Mariological' question that is discussed, and about which there is obviously vigorous contention, in the later fourth century, concerns Mary's perpetual virginity, her ἀειπαρθενία. Already Origen, as we have seen, had expressly demanded it, and it is clear that, even before Athanasius, the doctrine had come to be taken as a matter of course. Elsewhere it had not developed by any means so far. The radical, critical Arians such as Eudoxius and Eunomius disapproved of the perpetual virginity all along,[4] and the cautious discussions that *Basil* the Great devotes to this subject

[1] For the West one may refer in the same sense to Pseudo-Cyprian, *De singularitate clericorum*; Koch, *Virgo Eva*, 73f. Here the turning-point comes only with Ambrose; see pp. 76ff. below.

[2] Cf. G. Söll, 'Die Mariologie der Kappadokier im Licht der Dogmengeschichte', *TQ* 131 (1951, 163–88; 288–319; 426–57), 440ff. He says rightly on p. 434, 'It cannot be proved from the texts so far discovered that the Cappadocians laid any special stress on the ethical valuation of the Mother of God.' The attempt to go further by 'logical' considerations is historically uninteresting. Söll also brings Amphilochius into his researches, and in doing so he proceeds more cautiously and correctly than I. Ortiz de Urbina in 'Mariologia Amphilochii Iconiensis', *Orientalia Christiana Periodica* 23 (1957), 186–91.

[3] I hope that a dissertation that I have prompted will support these statements more fully. The exposition by R. P. Dieu, 'La mariologie de S. Jean Chrysostome' in *Mémoires et Rapports du Congrès Marial* 1 (Brussels, 1921), 71–83, is inadequate. On the other hand, it is, of course, quite fantastic when E. Michaud, 'La christologie de S. Jean Chrysostome', *Revue internationale de Théologie* 17 (1909, pp. 275–91), 282, considers the possibility that Chrysostom did not regard Mary as a virgin at all, but as a barren young wife.

[4] Philostorgius, *HE* VI 2.

show that it was not generally acknowledged, even in orthodox circles.[1] Basil was concerned, as always, to avoid any unnecessary accentuation of hostilities between rival parties in the sphere of Church law. He emphasizes that the acceptance of Mary's perpetual virginity is not really necessary. A dogmatic judgment that simply maintained her virginity up to the birth of Jesus would be adequate, and thanks to the positive testimony in Matthew this fact remains all along beyond discussion. But Basil adds at once that the assertion that the Mother of God ever ceased to be a virgin could not well be tolerated by devout Christians—it was, in a current expression used in the Roman Catholic Church of today, and here anticipated almost word for word, '*piis auribus offensibile*'.[2] Thus Basil looks afresh for proof that the apparently evidential arguments from Scripture need not necessarily be understood in that sense, and he lands back in the theory of the 'stepbrothers'—that is, he moves in the succession of Origen.[3] Other theologians now proceed more vigorously,[4] and so at last a denial of the perpetual virginity generally appears as a theological absurdity and an impossibility.[5] The final stage of the development is reached with *Epiphanius*. In the traditional style of the fight against heretics, he constructs for himself a sect of 'Antidicomarianites', who, of course, can have been induced only by the most sinister motives to defame the holy Virgin by casting doubt on her perpetual virginity.[6] And as on the other hand he knows of a no less reprehensible circle of women, the so-called

---

[1] The position of Apollinarius cannot be determined with complete certainty: Koch, *Virgo Eva*, 83, n. 1; but cf. *fr.* 2 in Reuss, *Matthäus-Kommentare*, 1.

[2] *Hom. in Christi gener.* 5: ἡμεῖς δέ, εἰ καὶ μηδὲν τῷ τῆς εὐσεβείας παραλυμαίνεται λόγῳ (μέχρι γὰρ τῆς κατὰ τὴν οἰκονομίαν ὑπηρεσίας ἀναγκαία ἡ παρθενία, τὸ δ' ἐφεξῆς ἀπολυπραγμόνητο τῷ λόγῳ τοῦ μυστηρίου), ὅμως διὰ τὸ μὴ καταδέχεσθαι τῶν φιλοχρίστων τὴν ἀκοήν, ὅτι ποτὲ ἐπαύσατο εἶναι παρθένος ἡ θεοτόκος, ἐκείνας ἡγούμεθα τὰς μαρτυρίας αὐτάρκεις.

[3] His attitude to apocryphal works is similarly cautious.

[4] So Gregory of Nyssa in a Christmas sermon (PG 46, 1140f.; Söll, 436); cf. Didymus, *Trin.* III 4. But it can hardly be said that in this text Gregory is also virtually 'teaching' the *virginitas in partu*. In the sentence in 1141 B καὶ ἡ μετὰ τόκου παρθένος, ἡ ἄφθορος μήτηρ περιέπει τὸ ἔκγονον the predicate ἄφθορος must not be interpreted physiologically in the sense of the 'incorruptibiliter' of *Can.* 3, with which the Lateran Council of 649 dogmatized the *virginitas in partu* for the Roman Catholic Church.

[5] But not only the reality of the birth, but also Mary's virginity has to be defended further against the Manichaeans, e.g. by Titus of Bostra: Sickenberger, *Titus*, 257f.

[6] *Haer.* LXXVIII.

Collyridians, who offer cakes to Mary and form a cult that is in some degree pagan,[1] he can present his standpoint as the happy medium between the extremes.[2]

The information gives us an inkling of the pressure to which the post-Constantinian Church was exposed from below as early as the fourth century, when, in spite of the praise and ascetic idealizing that had been bestowed on the figure of Mary in the meantime, it still held fast to the old and fundamentally human estimation of her person, and did not indulge in any direct veneration of her. In fact, the fourth century knows as yet no churches dedicated to Mary, no images of her, not one festival in her honour, and no liturgical invocation of Mary in the church service.[3] In contrast to some martyr saints, Mary is very much in the background. A changed attitude can be seen first in the outer territories of the eastern Church, outside the area where Greek was spoken. Here we must refer in particular to a piece of writing by *Athanasius*, preserved in Coptic, on virginity, though it may remain an open question whether this work was later tampered with in a 'popular' sense, or is actually authentic.[4] In the latter case it would make public the 'other' side of the great prelate, who is known to have preached in Coptic, and who was probably familiar with the wishes of the people that he

[1] *Haer.* LXXVIII, 23. 3–5;LXXIX. On this cf. F. J. Dölger, 'Die eigenartige Marienverehrung der Philomarianiten oder Kollyridianer in Arabien' in *Antike u. Christentum* 1 (1929), 107–42.

[2] *Haer.* LXXVIII 23.2f.; LXXIX 1.3f.

[3] Thus far D. Franses, 'Marienvereering en de erste euuw van de Kerk', *Collectancee Franciscana Neerlandica* V 3 (1941), who takes into account only the time up to the middle of the fourth century, is in my opinion right, in spite of the objection of Söll, *Kappadokier*, 456f., n. 13.

[4] Besides this there are two shorter texts to be considered, both of which have been edited by L.-Th. Lefort in *CSCO* 150/151 (1955). Neither has been preserved in its entirety. In judging of their authenticity I may be allowed to follow an expert, C. Detlef G. Müller, who has been kind enough to advise me. The short first text, which is generally regarded as authentic (the *Letter to Virgins*), and the questionable second one (*Precepts for Virgins*) with its list of Old Testament heroes and its praise of virginity, have no special interest for us. The decisive text is the large third one, which has no title, asserts the perpetual virginity of the θεοτόκος, and exhibits her to us as a model of ascetic virtues for virgins. As the text is attested by Shenoute and Ephraem and is used by Ambrose in his work on virgins, it must have been current before 376. Its authenticity is in general accepted by Coptic scholars, but is flatly contested by Arthur Vööbus, *History of Asceticism in the Syrian Orient* 1 (CSCO Subsidia 14, 1958), 64f. That might be going too far, but one has to reckon with the possibility of later enlargements and revisions.

knew how to guide.[1] Here Mary, as a virgin and the Mother of God, plays a part that goes perceptibly beyond what Athanasius says as a dogmatist and is in the habit of supporting elsewhere in his ascetic treatises.[2] Mary appears simply as the original and present model of ascetic living.[3] Already the apostle Paul is said to have set his course by her,[4] and her exemplary conduct is generally taken as 'a great help'.[5] Clearly, therefore, Mary has here taken the place hitherto occupied by Christ.

But in the region of eastern Syria, too, there is already at this time a personality of intellectual stature, who gives potent expression in numerous utterances (less strictly theological than rhetorical and poetic) to a new and enhanced veneration of Mary.[6] This is the Syrian teacher and poet *Ephraem*, who was born in Nisibis and died in 373 in Edessa in the border territory of the old empire. Ephraem

---

[1] But one must be careful not to be too ready to take the 'popular' religiosity as being specially ascetic and devoutly Marian. How little that is so for Egypt is shown by the *History of Joseph the Carpenter*, which originated there towards the end of the fourth century. In it Mary receives little attention, and does not appear as an ascetic. She is given into Joseph's care till her marriage (3.2), and her stepdaughters by Joseph's first wife marry 'as it is laid down for everyone' (11.1). In 20.1 she is bluntly described as 'simple': S. Morenz, *Die Geschichte von Joseph dem Zimmermann* (1951), 101.

[2] Here, too, questions of authenticity are much disputed; cf. the summary in H. Quasten, *Patrology* 3 (1960), 45ff. We can leave detailed discussion of these on one side, as the 'Mariological' pronouncements are not very fundamental in any of the relevant texts. The Λόγος σωτηρίας πρὸς τὴν παρθένον edited by E. von der Goltz (TU 29.2a [1905]) makes only one single quasi-credal mention of Mary (in ch. 3). The *Letter to the Virgins who have gone to Jerusalem*, edited by Lebon, *Muséon* 41 (1928), 170ff., refers to Mary, 'who was without water when she abode in the desert' (179), and so uses her as an example merely for the dispensability of washing-water. And the text of a further Λόγος περὶ παρθενίας, also edited by Lebon, *Muséon* 40 (1927), 209ff., incompletely in Syriac, and by Casey, *Sitzungsberichte der Berliner Akademie* 33 (1935), 1026ff., in Armenian, does indeed name a long list of biblical witnesses for virginity (Elijah, Elisha, Daniel and his companions, Jeremiah, Miriam, Zipporah, John the Baptist, John the Evangelist, Paul and Thecla), but for all that does not single out Mary as an example (200).

[3] § 135.   [4] § 95.   [5] § 124.

[6] It is the 'predilection for images, parallels, and antitheses, for types in nature and Scripture, which gives his speech poetic beauty, but his theology an indefiniteness that can hardly be reproduced in exact concrete terms': E. Beck, 'Die Mariologie der echten Schriften Ephräms', *Oriens christianum* 40 (1956), pp. 22–39), 38. In addition there is the difficulty of determining the authenticity of the voluminous quantity of material, which has been transmitted in various languages. Cf. the orientation by Beck in art. 'Ephrem le Syrien' in *Dictionnaire de Spiritualité* 4 (1960), 788–800 (798f.: 'Dévotion à Marie').

is 'virtually uninfluenced' by the outlook of 'the great contemporary Greek theologians',[1] and this judgment is also valid as regards the whole orientally profuse style of his poetic glorification of Mary as virgin and as Christ's mother and bride.[2] Here the old Eve-Mary typology has awakened to new and luxuriant life, and blossoms in an astonishing way. It is even said once that only Christ and his mother are without blemish or sin—in contrast to all other human beings and particularly to the refractory 'children' of the church of Edessa, whose sins Ephraem laments.[3] But if we look more closely, these terms really contain no assertion of Mary's absolute sinlessness. The way in which Ephraem envisages her sanctification is rather that in her conception of Christ through the Holy Spirit the Virgin at the same time received her 'baptism' and the gift of perfect purity.[4] Moreover, Mary does not yet appear, even in Ephraem, as a direct model for men and women ascetics. It is still rather Christ alone who prefers to live in the bodies of chaste (that is, ascetic) men and women, just as he once came down into a virgin.[5]

We do not follow the Church's development in the East beyond the fourth century. It produced step by step an increasingly rich

[1] So Beck, art. 'Ephräm' in *LTK* 3, 928; cf. art. 'Ephraem Syrus', *RAC* V (520–31), 524ff. Conversely one cannot 'speak of an influence of Ephraem's writings on the dogmatic development of fourth- and fifth-century Mariology'; L. Hammersberger, *Mariologie der ephremischen Schriften*, 37; cf. Söll, *Kappadokier*, 169.

[2] Up to a point he was anticipated in this by the gnostic *Odes of Solomon*, which may have been written first in Syriac: A. Adam, 'Die ursprüngliche Sprache der Salomo-Oden', *ZNW* 52 (1961), 141–56. On the title 'bride' see p. 60, n. 2, above.

[3] *Carm. Nisib.* 27.8.

[4] Beck, 'Mariologie', 26ff. Juan M. Fernandez, 'San Efrén Siro primer cantor de la immaculada concepción', *Humanidades* 10 (1958), 243–64, is much less cautious in his formulations. Nor do the Greek theologians of the following period go beyond Ephraem's views on this point—e.g. Chrysippus of Jerusalem (d. 479) in a sermon on Mary (PO 19, 338): O. Stegmüller, art. 'Chrysipp' in *LMK* I 6, 1149. The same may be said, too, of John of Damascus, as has rightly been shown, though with some qualification, by Grumel, *Mariologie de S. Jean Damascène*, 321ff., against C. Chevalier.

[5] *Carm. Nisib.* 46.1 (in Beck, 'Mariologie', 37). The same basic outlook is already shown by the pseudo-Clementine *Epistulae ad virgines*. Koch, *Virgo Eva*, 74ff., draws special attention to I 6 (F. X. Funk, *Patres Apostolici*, 3rd ed. by F. Diekamp, 1913, II, 9): 'A virgin's womb received our Lord Jesus Christ, the God Logos; and the body that our Lord bore and with which he carried on his conflict in this world, he had received from a [holy] virgin,< and after our Lord had become a human being in a virgin, he kept to this mode of life in this world>.'

development of Marian devotion and veneration, whose justification belongs to the general theology of the veneration of saints and images. Dogmatically, however, it scarcely led—of itself—to anything new beyond the doctrines characterized by the Alexandrian-Athanasian terms *aeiparthenos* and *theotokos*.[1] In this development the Mariological element in the title *theotokos* was originally hardly stressed at all. The confirmation of the title in the church dedicated to Mary at Ephesus in 431 had only Christological and no recognizable Mariological significance—at any rate if one has regard to the opinion of responsible churchmen.[2] The only eulogy that Cyril is said to have pronounced in Mary's honour at the Council[3] is in all

---

[1] Ortiz de Urbina, *Lo sviluppo della Mariologia*, 42, rightly says: 'One would not be far wrong if one were to say that the Mariology of the eastern fathers is for the most part in a fragmentary state,' and laments this 'lack of theological development of Mariology'; similarly M. Gordillo, *Mariologia orientalis* (OCA 141, 1954). This (in their opinion) 'fragmentary' character of orthodox Mariology easily misleads Roman Catholic critics into closing the gaps logically on the lines of their own theology. Even if the material for it is carefully collected from Greek writers, the conclusions are strange. Thus people even try to show the *immaculata conceptio* as an old tradition of the Greek fathers: M. Jugie, *L'immaculée conception dans l'écriture sainte et dans la tradition orientale* (Rome, 1952). The same holds good for Mary as mediator; thus—appealing to the Eve-Mary parallelism—M. Gordillo, 'La mediazione di Maria Vergine nella teologia bizantina', *Revue des études byzantines* 11 (1953), 120-8. On the *virginitas in partu* see below, pp. 71ff.

[2] This also follows—not quite in the author's sense—from the well-documented presentation by A. Eberles, *Die Mariologie des Hl. Cyrillus von Alexandrien* (1921). Certainly the Council of 431 may provide a certain turning-point in so far as its Christological decision indicated a welcome point of contact for the incipient Marian cult and the popular Marian devotion. The development is thus seen, for instance, by G. A. Wellen, *Theotokos—eine ikonographische Abhandlung über das Gottesmutterbild in frühchristlicher Zeit* (Utrecht-Antwerp 1960), 94: 'From the Council of Ephesus onwards the person of the Mother of God gains more and more in importance both in theological thought and <also> in the cult. Up to then her name was mentioned in treatises and in preaching only when the person of Christ aroused thought of his mother. But the thoughts are now directed straight to her person, although they are inseparably bound up with Christ. And the veneration . . . now appears in the public life of the Church.' It is from this angle that we must see the establishment of the first Roman church dedicated to Mary, Santa Maria Maggiore, by Sixtus III (432-40). But on p. 118 Wellen rightly warns us against a one-sided emphasis on the Mariological meaning of its mosaics (as they were represented, e.g. by G. Stuhlfauth, 'Zu Ehren der Gottesmutter', *Theologische Blätter* 5 [1926], 301-3). The Council was, in fact, 'dedicated above all to the person of Christ, and the triumphal arch in Santa Maria Maggiore is primarily evidence of the orthodox doctrine on the *adventus domini*' (p. 129).

[3] *Acta conc. oecum.* I 32, pp. 102-4, *coll. Vatic.* 80 = *Hom. div.* 4.

probability not authentic but a later forgery.[1] It is not till after Cyril's time that Mary rises in status unmistakably above all the saints,[2] even the apostles not excepted.[3] Nor did the doctrine of Mary's ἀειπαρθενία lead to a closer dogmatic definition of the need for a virgin birth. Only to those of a certain religious turn of mind can it seem convincing with no further argument that none but the purest, perpetually intact virgin could form a worthy house for the celestial divine man.[4] But the virgin birth itself is now no longer regarded in the old anti-docetic sense as a sign of Jesus' true humanity, but— as had already begun with Athanasius[5]—is valued above all as a sign of his full divinity, whose holiness seems commensurate with such a miracle.[6]

[1] H. Dörries, *Göttingische gelehrte Anzeigen* 192 (1930), 380ff.; cf. A. d'Alès, *Recherches de science religieuse* 22 (1932), 62–70. E. Schwartz remarks briefly and pertinently in his edition: 'sermo non est Cyrilli.' In spite of this the Migne text is happily quoted again and again and brought out as welcome evidence of Cyril's Mariology, e.g. by Söll, 'Maria-Kirche', p. 139; Huhn, 'Maria est typus ecclesiae secundum patres' (see p. 78, n. 7, below), 199; and A. Spindeler, art. 'Kyrill von Alexandrien', *LTK* 6, 708. Even J. Quasten, *Patrology* 3 (1960), 131, treats it unhesitatingly as authentic, and notices Schwartz's divergent standpoint only in the summary of literature on p. 132.

[2] But in the Council of Chalcedon Mariology still occupied 'only a modest place': H. Riedinger, art. 'Chalcedon' in *LMK* I 6, 1091. Most of the relevant statements are found, characteristically, in the *Tome of Leo*—that is, in a western document.

[3] See p. 61 above.

[4] The ascetic logic of Pseudo-Justin (see above, pp. 56–57) can now be in some degree inverted to support this idea: already Cyril of Jerusalem infers from the cultic chastity of the priests, which is taken as a matter of course, the inevitability of a virgin birth of their Lord, *Cat.* XII 25 (PG 33, 757): ἔπρεπε γὰρ τῷ ἁγιωτάτῳ καὶ διδασκάλῳ ἐξ ἁγνῶν ἐξεληλυθέναι παστάδων. εἰ γὰρ ὁ τῷ Ἰησοῦ καλῶς ἱερατεύων ἀπέχεται γυναικός, αὐτὸς ὁ Ἰησοῦς πῶς ἔμελλεν ἐξ ἀνδρὸς καὶ γυναικὸς ἔρχεσθαι;

[5] See p. 63, n. 4 above.

[6] Cf. Eberle, *op. cit.*, pp. 73, 105, 116. But the *virginitas in partu*, inferred here from the painless birth, is not thus expressed by Cyril himself.

IV

Later Dogmatic Developments
in the West

IT IS only in the West that the early Church pushes the development of the problems beyond this rather indeterminate state, and it is to the West that we must now turn. In the second half of the fourth century the Latin Church begins to take rapid strides to make good the gap between its development and that of the East. New problems of ecclesiology and anthropology are stirred up, and from the specifically western point of view of man's original sin stemming from Adam the doctrine of the virgin birth, too, acquires a changed meaning which takes up and broadens the earlier understanding of it.

Till then the West, even in ascetic writings, had been cautious about any glorification of Mary. Apocryphal writings were received sceptically; no old Latin translation of the *Protevangelium of James* seems to have existed at all. Accordingly the idea of Mary's 'eternal' virginity is also absent. At any rate, up to and including *Lactantius* there is no certain Latin evidence for the affirmation of the doctrine, and *Victorinus* of Pettau still seems to have spoken quite naturally of the brothers that Jesus had.[1] One may perhaps cite *Firmicus Maternus*, for he once designates Mary as 'virgo Dei'.[2] Ever since Tertullian and Cyprian this has been the well-established term for the Church's virgins who are dedicated to God and pledged to perpetual virginity.[3] But even *Hilary* of Poitiers, who in his

---

[1] Helvidius refers to him, and Jerome's protest against such an interpretation, *Adv. Helv.* 17, is unconvincing: Koch, *Adhuc Virgo*, pp. 27f.; *Virgo Eva* pp. 82f.; otherwise Blinzler, *Brüder des Herrn*, 245, n. 123.
[2] *De errore prof. rel.* 25.2; on this see Koch, *Virgo Eva*, 81.
[3] We have to be content with this rather uncertain and indirect evidence. Koch, *Virgo Eva*, 81, refers beyond it to the *Consultatio Zacchaei et Apollonii*, which in c. 11 even expressly emphasizes the *virginitas in partu*. But this work, as is now established, is not by Firmicus, but did not originate till after 411: B. Altaner, *Patrologie* (1960⁶), 324f.

Commentary on Matthew is the first resolutely to uphold Mary's eternal virginity, has to defend it against numerous impious people who appeal against it to the text of Matthew's Gospel and will therefore have none of the new 'spiritual doctrine'.[1]

It is not till the second half of the fourth century that the whole question comes fully to life,[2] as the new monastic enthusiasm for the ideal of virginity spreads over from the East into the West.[3] Just because asceticism in the West had so far played a natural but only limited role, the strange enthusiasm and radicalism of the new piety at first ran into strong opposition and set off reactions. Here, in contrast to the East, the question of Mary and her virginity very soon assumes a special importance. Indeed, Helvidius, Jovinian, and later Bonosus sought to meet the overvaluation of the ascetic ideal partly by appealing, in line with the older western tradition, to Mary's later, natural marriage with Joseph.[4] Thereupon in opposition to this Ambrose, Jerome and many others put forth the new doctrine of the ἀειπαρθενία and upheld it passionately. The words of Scripture no longer avail against it; anyone who brings them into action against the eternal virginity merely proves thereby, as Jerome says ironically, that though he may read, he cannot understand 'what, to a devout conviction, remains unshaken'.[5] But not content with that, one can now bring the ἀειπαρθενία to bear on the abstruse idea of Mary's immaculate physical intactness continuing even during the birth. This pretentious theological discovery of a *virginitas* not only *ante* and *post partum*, but also

[1] *Comm. Matt.* I 3: 'sed plures irreligiosi et a spiritali doctrina admodum alieni occasionem ex eo occupant turpiter de Maria opinandi, quod dictum sit . . .' (Matt. 1.18, 20, 25). The *Commentary on Matthew* was written before Hilary was exiled to the East; but, of course, that does not exclude the possibility of eastern influences: Koch, *Virgo Eva*, 79ff.

[2] Thus also J. Galot, 'La virginité de Marie et la naissance de Jésus', *Nouv. Rev. théol.* 82 (1960), 449–69.

[3] In what follows cf. especially the sound presentation by P. Friedrich, 'St Ambrosius über die Jungfrauengeburt Marias (virginitas Mariae in partu)', *Festgabe Alois Knöpfler* (1917) 89–109.

[4] But it is only the *virginitas in partu*, and not also *post partum*, that Jovinian is clearly alleged to have contested; cf. Ambrose, *Ep.* 42.2: 'uirgo concepit, sed non virgo generauit'.

[5] *Adv. Helvid.* 2: 'ipsis quibus aduersum nos usus est testimoniis reuincatur, ut intelligat se et legere potuisse, quae scripta sunt, et non potuisse, quae pietate roborata sunt, cognoscere.' But Ambrose does not, any more than Jerome, refrain from a detailed rectification of the supposedly false expositions: *Inst. virg.* 5.36–9.57.

in partu, is specially to the credit of Latin theologians.[1] It reminds

[1] Perhaps the first western witness to describe circumstantially the miraculous painless birth and Mary's perpetual physical intactness is Zeno of Verona in his sermons delivered in 362–72. In these he obviously depends on the account in the *Protevangelium of James*, but he already shows the characteristic emphasis on the three phases of the virginity set side by side: 'ceterum fuit illa uirgo post connubium, uirgo post conceptum, uirgo post filium' (*Tract.* I 5.3; cf. II 8.2).

It is usual in this context to refer to Hilary of Poitiers. Even Hugo Koch (*Adhuc Virgo*, p. 29) is of the opinion that *De trinitate* III 19 (PL 10, 87) assumes the *virginitas in partu*, with which Hilary had obviously become acquainted 'during his involuntary stay in the East (356–359)'. 'According to the whole connected sequence—it speaks of the Father's having suffered no *damnum* through the begetting of the Son—the *virginitas in partu* is certainly not meant alone, or even primarily; but it is meant to be included.' Now it may certainly be dangerous to argue on the basis of a text of which no critical edition is yet available; but I think I can show that even this cautious formulation by Koch goes too far.

In the assertions under discussion it is, in fact, indispensable to consider 'the whole connected sequence' if we are to understand them properly. Taking up an anti-Arian position, Hilary first emphasizes that in the Son the whole fullness of the Father dwelt bodily (Col. 2.9) (III 15), and that according to John 17.4 the Father was first revealed to us through him (III 16). 'Nam deum nemo noscit, nisi confiteatur et patrem unigeniti filii et filium non de portione aut dilatione aut emissione, sed ex eo natum inenarrabiliter, incomprehensibiliter ut filium a patre plenitudinem diuinitatis, ex qua et in qua natus est, obtinentem, uerum et infinitum et perfectum deum; haec enim Dei est plenitudo' (III 17). The point is that this inexpressible birth should be believed.' The Son himself performed his miracles on earth—the changing of water into wine and the feeding of the multitude are specially mentioned—in order to make us certain about the birth: 'uolens itaque filius huius natiuitatis suae fidem facere factorum suorum nobis posuit exemplum, ut per inenarrabilium gestorum suorum inenarrabilem efficientiam de uirtute natiuitatis doceremur.' A direct perception of the divine mystery is denied to us, 'quibus intelligentia ad conspicabiles res et corporeas coarctatur'; but if we hold to the visible miracle, we can also affirm the incomprehensible. For the Son is the Father's image: 'cum enim sensu atque uerbis imaginem apprehendimus, necesse est etiam eum, cuius imago est, consequamur.' But we do not cease to make our foolish and wicked demands for the invisible, 'quomodo filius et unde filius et quo damno patris uel ex qua portione sit natus', instead of keeping to the evidential *exempla operationum* (III 18). Instead of embarking on those injudicious questions, one should therefore cite further miracles which elucidate them indirectly, and which, although just as incomprehensible, were actually experienced in Jesus' life: 'quaeris, quomodo secundum spiritum natus sit filius; ego te de corporeis rebus interrogo' (III 19).

So far the context is clear; we must simply not bring the 'secundum spiritum' (κατὰ πνεῦμα) into contact with the virgin birth through the Spirit, but must always relate the words to the divine eternal birth of the Son from the Father. This holds good in just the same way for the further example of the passage of Christ's risen body through the closed doors (John 20.19). This picture is eagerly brought in later to illuminate the miracle of the *uterus clausus*; the earliest western example that I know of is in Rufinus, *Comm. symb.* 9. In the relevant

73

passage, however, the miracle is again used only to give mundane corroboration of the supramundane miracle of the divine birth: 'adstitit dominus clauso domo in medio discipulorum—et filius est natus ex patre, noli negare, quod steterit, quia per intelligentiae infirmitatem consistentis non consequaris introitum— noli nescire, quod ab ingenito et perfecto deo patre unigenitus et perfectus filius deus natus sit, quia sensum et sermonem humanae naturae uirtus generationis excedat' (III 20).

Now in between there is in III 19 a short section which also brings in Jesus' virgin birth as a further earthly miracle that is to substantiate the miracle of the divine birth. This view again puts the closing formula beyond doubt: 'et quidem fas esset, non impossibile in deo opinari, quod per uirtutem eius possibile fuisse in homine cognoscimus.' But in what does the analogy of the miraculous between the heavenly and the earthly birth consist? Obviously in this: that just as God experienced no diminution through the begetting of a son, although he had brought him forth out of his own nature, so Mary had no co-operation from a man, and yet brought forth a complete human being without thereby diminishing her own nature: 'et certe non suscepit, quod edidit, sed caro carnem sine elementorum nostrorum pudore prouexit et perfectum ipsa de suis non imminuta generauit.' There is no meditation here on the detailed circumstances of a supposedly painless birth without loss of blood and so on; the point of the miracle is rather that Mary 'received' nothing from outside and could yet, as a complete human being, bring forth a complete human being. The phrase 'sine elementorum nostrorum pudore' refers to the sexual act which otherwise is necessary for the begetting of a human being, but which here did not take place; cf. *Tract. psalm.* LXVII (Zingerle, CSEL 22 [1891], 301): 'quia ipsae illae corporum et elementorum nostrorum origines sint pudendae.' I cannot find according to this, as Koch claims, *op. cit.*, 29, n. 1, that in particular Tertullian's view 'that the process of Jesus' birth in relation to the *pudenda* did not differ from other births (*Adv. Marc.* III 11; IV 21; *De carne Christi* 4)' was negatived in the sense of a *virginitas in partu*. For up to now our text has not been at all about a *virginitas in partu*. It is a question now whether this was so in the preceding sentence that connects with the introductory sentence quoted earlier. We may repeat the latter here: 'quaeris quomodo secundum spiritum natus sit filius; ego te de corporeis rebus interrogo. non (?) quaero, quomodo natus ex uirgine sit, an detrimentum sui caro perfectam ex se carnem generans perpessa sit. et certe non suscepit', etc. It is a question whether the 'non' of the traditional text can remain, and in my opinion that is not the case. But even if we keep the negation, the sentence still does not contain the clear affirmation of a *virginitas in partu* idea that one would like to find in it. Let us substantiate this first.

Non quaero—that means, therefore, that Hilary has no wish to discuss in greater detail the mysteries, the *quomodo*, of the virgin birth from Mary. Especially he does not wish to go into the question whether or not her 'flesh' suffered injury through it. That would mean, in my opinion, that Hilary, as well as Zeno soon afterwards, already knows the Greek story of the miraculous birth in the *Protevangelium of James*, but that—as was once the case with Clement of Alexandria (see p. 55 above)—he does not want to enter into a more detailed discussion of those statements. Such an attitude would be all the more understandable, as the comparison would hardly have yielded anything serviceable for what he had in mind; for the 'damnum' of a diminution of God's substance as father does not provide a good comparison with the injury done to a virgin's body through a birth. What is conclusive is that a new comone of gnostic myths,[1] but hardly has anything to do with them directly. For the Greeks such an idea was to some extent included in the acknowledgment of the 'eternal' virginity of the Mother of God; but it had never been made an independent theme of theological reflection and arguments such as are now beginning in the West and, however painfully, are continued with clumsy *naïveté* into the Middle Ages and beyond.[2] In them the ascetic evaluation of the virgin birth seems so much a matter of course that, e.g., Pope *Siricius* sees the dogma itself in danger if a later conjugal cohabitation between Joseph and Mary should be even considered.[3] After *Gaudentius* the divine birth even enhanced the resplendence of

---

plete Being appears beside the old one without the latter's having become 'less' on that account or having received anything from outside. One could therefore hardly say, even if the traditional text were retained, that the *virginitas in partu* is 'meant to be included' in this passage. Rather is it left aside without discussion, asking a question that Hilary will not tackle, while, apart from this passage, he has nowhere even touched on it.

Really, however, in spite of the Maurists' objection, we must agree with Lipsius who would delete the 'non'. Only thus do we get a completely plain and coherent argument without unnecessary sidelong glances, and the steady and impressive contrasting of the earthly with the incomprehensible heavenly event is preserved. In contrast to the 'speculating' Arians Hilary will not speak of high and heavenly things, but contents himself with looking at the miracle of Christ's earthly birth. Here, too, it came about that a being—Mary—brought forth from herself a second Being, although—in contrast to what is ordinarily necessary—nothing came to her for this from outside; yet she remained whole in herself—not uninjured in the physical sense; and that exactly corresponds to the miracle of the heavenly birth of the Logos from God, about whom also we are therefore to have no doubts. If this text and its exposition are correct, therefore, Hilary must be entirely eliminated as an early western witness for the idea of a *virginitas in partu*.

[1] See pp. 23 and 54, n. 2; Karl Adam, 'Theologische Bemerkungen zu Hugo Kochs Schrift: *Virgo Eva—Virgo Maria* 1937', *TQ* 119 (1938, 171–89), 177, n. 1; K. Rahner, 'Virginitas in partu', p. 190.

[2] A comprehensive survey of the position taken by the fathers and of the recent literature on this problem is provided in particular by Karl Rahner with his 'Beitrag zum Problem der Dogmenentwicklung und Überlieferung'. Perhaps these old and long since forgotten controversies may help to explain the custom —strange, having regard to the Bible—that even today with reference to the confession of faith we speak of the virgin *birth* instead of a virgin *conception* of Jesus—a circumstance to which Herr Habs and Herr Reicke specially drew my attention in the discussion of this lecture in the Academy.

[3] Siricius, *Ep.* 9.3: 'qui enim hoc astruit, nihil aliud nisi perfidiam Iudaeorum astruit, qui dicunt eum non potuisse nasci ex uirgine, nam si hanc accipiant a sacerdotibus auctoritatem, ut uideatur Maria partus fudisse plurimos, maiore studio ueritatem fidei expugnare contendent.'

Mary's intactness.[1] It is still more characteristic that *Jerome* regards it as commanded that Joseph, too, should be preserved for the ideal of virginity.[2] He therefore condemns the theory, so long predominant, that Jesus' brothers were his stepbrothers from a previous marriage, and maintains that on the contrary, according to the usage of biblical language, they must have been his cousins.[3] That arbitrary assumption had the further advantage that it freed the theory of Mary's eternal virginity from the testimony of the apocryphal source, the only place where anything was to be read about the 'stepbrothers' and Joseph's widowhood. This may have been one of the main reasons why Jerome's theory came to be acknowledged comparatively quickly in the West, while the East stuck to the older apocryphal basis.[4]

However characteristic all this may be, it brings, all in all, no new ideas into the discussions, and does not go in any positive or material way beyond the Greek view of the virgin birth. It is not till Ambrose connects the question of the virgin birth with the problem of original sin that a decisive step forward is taken.

Of all the early fathers the most productive and interesting from 'Marian' points of view is undoubtedly *Ambrose*.[5] He combines

[1] Gaudentius, *Tract.* XIII 4 (Glueck, CSEL 68 [1936], 115): 'hanc omnipotentiam filii dei et hominis etiam mater uirgo testatur, quae de spiritu sancto concipiens ita deum et hominem, quem pudico utero gestauerat, edidit, ut apud incorruptam tanti nominis matrem post diuinum partum gloriosior integritas permaneret'; similarly IX 12.

[2] *The Mariology of St Jerome* was treated some time ago by Joh. Nissen (Diss. theol. Münster, 1913); however, this work does not represent much more than a quantity of material industriously assembled and slightly confused at times by the editor's own theological reflections. On this subject Jerome was not an original theologian. He collects a wide range of material, mostly obtained from the writings of Origen, and understands how to expand it from his own resources on occasion and use it in a fascinating way; cf. for instance in *C. Joh. Hieros.* 32 the consideration of the four kinds of human origin that have become a reality with Adam, Eve, Abel, and Christ. His ascetic preaching, which he had very much at heart, mostly centres in the old way on Christ alone. But against Jovinian he looks on Mary as the image and 'mother' of virgins: *Ep.* 22.38; *Adv. Jovin.* I 31: 'et tamen haec uirgo perpetua multarum est mater virginum.' In *Sermon* 159.1, which is today again regarded as authentic, he roundly declares after Origen (see p. 63), 'Maria uirgo mater domini inter mulieres principatum tenet.'

[3] *Adv. Helvid.* 11–17. For the exposition of the Gospel texts in detail cf. Koch, *Adhuc virgo*, p. 33, n. 2; 37.

[4] Cf. Zahn, 'Brüder und Vettern', *Forschungen* . . . 6, 320–25.

[5] For that very reason he may easily lead one to read more into his words than

all the stimulus provided by his astonishingly wide range of reading in Greek theological literature with the older western interests and traditions, and continues them independently. It is certainly true that he develops no 'Mariology' that exists and coheres of itself; but he is far more interested than his predecessors in Mary's person, and he repeatedly shows loving regard for her in his exegetical and practical writings. This interest is not traceable primarily to special dogmatic views—the 'Mother of God'[1] simply keeps here her old recognized place;[2] what is decisive is rather the new enthusiasm for the ascetic ideal of living, in the fight for which Ambrose played a leading and effective part all his life. In his sermons, and especially in his treatises designed for the 'virgins' of the community, he is never tired of praising and advocating the new heavenly and Christian virtue—surpassing all human wisdom—of virginity. Christ brought it into the world; but beside him it is now above all Mary, whose 'holy image summons all people to the service of virginity'.[3] For Ambrose she has become the most eminent and authoritative 'teacher of virginity'.[4] He is indignant that there are people, even bishops, who can doubt her perpetual

---

they contain. It is hopeless to try to use them in conjunction with modern terms such as co-operation in Christ's redemptive work, mediation, and the like, as has unfortunately been done by J. Huhn, to whom nevertheless we owe the most thorough presentation of this subject: *Das Geheimnis der Jungfrau-Mutter Maria nach dem Kirchenvater Ambrosius* (1954); cf. by the same author the article 'Ambrosius' in *LMK* I 1, 178-85. Ch. Neumann, *The Virgin Mary in the works of St Ambrose* (Diss. Fribourg, 1954), was not available to me.

[1] Ambrose calls Mary 'mater Dei' in *Exam.* V 65 and *Virg.* II 7; elsewhere for the most part only 'mater domini': Huhn, *Geheimnis*, p. 16.

[2] In the virgin's womb there was accomplished the 'contubernium diuinitatis et corporis sine ulla concretae confusionis labe' which is the ground of our salvation: *Virg.* I 3.13; cf. W. Seibel, *Fleisch und Geist beim hl. Ambrosius* (1958), 160f. Ambrose can still characterize the virgin birth in the old anti-docetic sense as a genuine human birth, 'quia homo uirgo' (*In ps.* XXXIX 18): 'partus uirginis non naturem mutauit' (*Incarn.* 104). But in general he is already moving decisively in the opposite, Athanasian direction, according to which it is not the actual but the miraculous birth that is stressed as a sign of the divine origin: 'talis decet partus deum' (line 4 of the hymn *Veni, Redemptor gentium*): Huhn, *Geheimnis*, 20ff., 74ff.

[3] *Inst. virg.* 5.35: . . . 'cum omnes ad cultum uirginitatis sanctae Mariae aduocentur exemplo.'

[4] *Inst. virg.* 6.45: 'uirginitatis magistra'. The 'mystical' images of the *virgo Maria* are also applied to her pupils: *ibid.* 9.58-62.

virginity,[1] and at a Milan synod he expressly has the ravenous wolves condemned whose madness finds incredible and rejects even the *virginitas in partu* alone.[2] The picture of Mary's life of virtue is warmly described and amplified. In explaining Luke's Gospel Ambrose, following the text, shows in particular Mary's humility and faith at the annunciation; but the highest reward has been granted to her for the sake of her chastity.[3] Certainly, Mary was only 'God's temple, not the temple's God', and if we must, in fact, worship the Holy Spirit as we do Christ, we must take care not to draw similar conclusions for the earthly mother, too.[4] But it was Mary who as a holy virgin was chosen to come from heaven 'to carry the forgiveness of sins in her womb',[5] and who as the new Eve[6] overcame the devil.[7] Although she remained completely passive

---

[1] *Inst. virg.* 5.35.

[2] *Ep.* 42. Moreover, in spite of his firm conviction of the *virginitas in partu*, even Ambrose can on occasion express himself inexactly and apparently contradictorily on this point: Koch, *Virgo Eva*, pp. 95f.; on this see the rectification by Huhn, *Geheimnis*, 125—materially correct, but unnecessarily indignant.

[3] *Inst. virg.* 6.45: 'et quae esset, cui maius quam matri dominus meritum reponeret, praemium reseruaret? nulli enim uberiora quam uirginitati deputauit munera, sicut scriptura nos docet.'

[4] *Spir. s.* III 79f.: 'haud dubie etiam sanctus spiritus adorandus est, quando adoratur ille, qui secundum carnem natus ex spiritu sancto est. ac ne quis hoc deriuet ad Mariam uirginem: Maria erat templum dei, non deus templi, et ideo ille solus adorandus, qui operabatur in templo.' Obviously Ambrose—like Epiphanius and Chrysostom—is trying here to obviate a danger that is already threatening. The first evidence for a prayer to Mary is in Gregory of Nazianzus, *Or.* 24.11 (*in laudem Cypriani*)—though it is in the framework of a popular legend of the chaste martyr Justina, who in her distress calls to Mary for help.

[5] *Inst. virg.* 13.81.

[6] With Ambrose the Eve-Mary typology comes from the western tradition; but as he now expounds it, on lines (like Philo's) that are more moral than typological, he gives it a new direction: Daniélou, *Sacramentum futuri*, 35. B. Capelle, *Le thème de la nouvelle Ève*, 56–62, provides a good collation and criticism of the material.

[7] *Obit. Theod.* 44. A critical inquiry into Ambrose's view of Mary's relationship to the Church does not come within our scope, though it would still be worth while. Ambrose is the first Church father in whose writings '*Maria*' and '*ecclesia*' occasionally come into more than purely accidental contact. This characterizes his position between the older fathers and the medieval development. His importance can therefore be fully recognized if we not only put his utterances carefully side by side with all the later ideas, and certainly all the modern ones, but also do not overvalue the supposed predecessors in this direction. See pp. 43f. above. Nor can Huhn, *Geheimnis*, 127ff.; pp. 144ff., and 'Maria est typus ecclesiae secundum patres, imprimis secundum S. Ambrosium et S. Augustinum' in *Maria et Ecclesia* (see p. 43, n. 1, above), 163–9, satisfy one in this respect.

at her conception, and the Lord had to complete his redemptive work alone without her co-operation, yet it began with Mary, and 'she through whom salvation was prepared for all men was to be the first to receive salvation from the fruit of her body'.[1]

In spite of his excessively eulogistic utterances about Mary's being 'freed from the burden of earthly failings',[2] Ambrose did not develop a firm theory of her sinlessness;[3] but the virgin birth is indeed to be viewed from this angle in so far as it becomes the means of guarding Christ himself from all defilement by original sin. Whereas all other human beings are sinners and 'conceived in sin', the virgin conception and birth of Christ actually proceeded from the beginning without defilement. Through them Christ remained guarded from the 'natural taint' of original sin. He, and he alone, was conceived 'not in impurity',[4] and thus he was born 'in pure joy'.[5] That means that the deciding factor in Christ's sinlessness is that he was not begotten 'in the usual way'. No one who originates through the bodily union of man and woman is free from sin; and conversely, 'only he who is free from sin is also free from this kind of begetting'.[6] This is an assertion that Ambrose repeatedly and

[1] *Exp. Luc.* II 17.

[2] *Exp. Luc.* X 42: 'quam terrena vitia non gravarent'; cf. *ibid.* II 28; 'quae nescit errorem'.

[3] Jos. Huhn, *Ursprung und Wesen des Bösen und der Sünde nach dem Kirchenvater Ambrosius* (1933), 109ff., and *Geheimnis*, 238ff., finds in him testimony only to personal sinlessness, not yet to freedom from original sin, although there is said already to be some approach towards the latter. That considerably restricts the assertions of older interpreters, but it goes too far. Quite apart from the question how far Ambrose's sharp scholastic distinction between personal and inherited sinfulness can be applied at all, it is not possible to turn occasional rhetorical laudations (see p. 79, n. 1) into a dogmatic theory that would absolutely contradict the oft-stressed Ambrosian doctrine of the universal sinfulness of man (Huhn, *Ursprung*, 104ff.) and would—as it were casually— exalt Mary to make her an exception on principle. This follows from the position of Augustine, who first reflected on the problem. See pp. 81f. below.

[4] Ps. 51.5 is a verse that Ambrose very often quotes directly and indirectly, e.g. *Apol. David* 56; *Paen.* I 3.13, continuing characteristically: 'Christi autem caro damnauit peccatum, quod nascendo non sensit, quod moriendo crucifixit.'

[5] In *In ps.* XXXVII 5 (Petschenig, CSEL 64 [1919], 139), Ambrose, proceeding from here, tries to make the expression 'similitudo peccati' (Rom. 8.3) intelligible: 'quia etsi naturalem substantiam carnis huius susceperat, nec in iniquitatibus conceptus et natus est in delictis (Ps. 51.5), qui non ex sanguinibus neque ex uoluntate carnis neque ex uoluntate uiri, sed de spiritu sancto natus (John 1.13) ex uirgine est.'

[6] Thus in the lost exposition of Isaiah, from which Augustine, *Contra duas epist. Pelagianorum* IV 29 (Urba and Zycha, CSEL 60 [1913], 559f.) quotes:

energetically worked out at different times in his life. It is peculiar to him. Feelings of 'natural' shyness about the domain of sex and the assertion of its direct connection with human sin are certainly found elsewhere, e.g. in Origen,[1] on whom Ambrose partly depends for his formulations.[2] But Ambrose goes far beyond him; the ascetic consideration of the 'flesh' widens into a fundamental reflection on the nature of sin; original sin comes out more clearly and decisively than it had ever done in the thought and doctrine of any eastern Church father. With this the ascetic understanding of Christ's virgin birth gains a directly dogmatic importance that it had hitherto lacked.

Here we are at a decisive point. Ambrose is not yet conscious of expressing a special dogmatic truth that will have to be defended against any possible contestants. But *Augustine* was completely justified later in appealing to Ambrose against the Pelagians,[3] and it was through Augustine that the idea then received its final form that determined the future.

Augustine, unlike Ambrose, is certainly not a theologian whose own thought and piety are determined by a 'Marian' outlook.[4]

' "idcirco Christus immaculatus, quia nec ipsa quidem nascendi solita conditione maculatus est". et alio loco in eodem opere loquens de apostolo Petro "ipse", inquit, "obtulit, quod ante putabat esse peccatum, lauacri sibi non solum pedes, sed et caput poscens, quod illico intellexisset lauacro pedum, qui in primo lapsi sunt homine, sordem obnoxiae successionis aboleri." item in eodem opere "seruatum est igitur", inquit, "ut ex uiro et muliere, id est per illam corporum commixtionem nemo uideatur expers esse delicti; qui autem expers delicti est, expers est etiam huiusmodi conceptionis." ' Here follows a further, lost quotation from *De Noe et arca*. Cf. further Augustine, *De nuptiis et concupiscentia* II 15; *Opus imperf.* IV 88, and Ambrose, *Exp. Luc.* II 56; *In ps.* CXVIII 6.22; *Virg.* I 21.

[1] Cf. especially *Hom. Lev.* VIII 3; XII 4; also Cyril of Jerusalem (p. 70, n. 4, above), and moreover H. Chadwick, art. 'Enkratiten', *RAC* V, col. 363.

[2] The passage quoted on p. 79, n. 5, above, from *In ps.* XXXVII 5 touches Origen closely, *Comm. Rom.* VI 12; Huhn, *Ursprung*, pp. 107f.

[3] Cf. J. Huhn, 'Ein Vergleich der Mariologie des Hl. Augustinus mit der des Hl. Ambrosius in ihrer Abhängigkeit, Ähnlichkeit, in ihrem Unterschied', *Augustinus Magister* I (Congrès internationale Augustinien, Paris, 1954), 221–39.

[4] This is not, of course, uncontested. In what follows I confine myself to the dogmatically decisive line. But it seems to me characteristic that in his idea of Mary Augustine never went beyond Ambrose in anything essential. He does not even call her 'mater Dei' as Ambrose does (F. Hofmann, following Friedrich [see next note] and against Huhn, *Geheimnis*, 16, is right on this point in his article. 'Augustinus' in *LMK* I 3/4 [456–69], 459), and avoided,

Apart from his sermons and occasional exegetical expositions he rarely came to speak about Mary of his own volition.[1] Most personal, perhaps, are his utterances before the community's virgins, whom he parallelizes with Mary. Augustine emphasizes the spiritual relationship and Mary's motherhood, which is not solely physical, and the position, as unique as it is symbolical, that Mary has for all believers and for every devout soul.[2] In the doctrine of the virgin birth he took over, as a matter of course, the results of earlier discussions—including the *virginitas in partu*—and defended them against heretics, particularly the Manichaeans, using on occasion the current apologetic arguments.[3] He is familiar with, and discusses, the problem of the genealogical trees as well as that of Jesus' brothers and sisters,[4] but he hardly adds anything new to it.[5] Nor was it

---

perhaps intentionally, the title 'bride' (Ambrose does not use this either): Capelle, *Le thème de la nouvelle Ève*, 71. In typology he always makes Adam and Eve correspond to Christ and the Church, not to Christ and Mary: Henri Rondet, 'Le Christ nouvel Adam dans la théologie de Saint Augustin', *BSFEM* 13 (1955, pp. 25–41), 41. Above all, he did not develop Mary's relationship to the Church: 'One cannot speak of an "equation" Mary—Church in Ambrose's writings', as is emphasized very suitably by Ildef. M. Dietz, 'Maria und die Kirche nach dem Hl. Augustinus', *Maria et ecclesia* (see p. 78, n. 7, above) (201–39), 218f., 'in opposition to Müller' (see p. 44, n. 1). As to 'Mary's place in the redemptive order according to St Augustine', cf. the excellent exposition by Fritz Hofmann in *Abhandlungen über Theologie und Kirche* (*Adam-Festschrift*, 1952), 213–24.

[1] Still fundamental, and often superior to more recent works, is Phil. Friedrich, *Die Mariologie des hl. Augustinus* (1907). A shorter survey of the relevant material is given by Hofmann (see previous note).

[2] *De s. virginitate* 5f. Modern interpretations like to start from texts of this kind about the 'maternitas spiritualis'; c.f., e.g., F. Hofmann, *Mariens Stellung*, pp. 218ff.; Huhn, 'Maria est typus Ecclesiae', 195ff.; Dietz, 'Maria und die Kirche', 222ff.

[3] Characteristically with Augustine, as with the Cappadocians (Söll, *Mariologie der Kappadokier*, 291), there is an almost complete absence of the natural and mythological analogies with the virgin birth: Friedrich, *Mariologie*, pp. 68f.; Huhn, *Mariologie bei Augustinus*, p. 227; cf. on this *Epp.* 137.2; 161.2. And Cyril of Jerusalem refers to them in *Cat.* XII 17 only with a slight apology. On the other hand, Rufinus, *Comm. symb.* 11, and especially Jerome, *Adv. Jov.* I 42, use them eagerly.

[4] Friedrich, *Mariologie*, pp. 19–47; 96–123.

[5] Nor does the idea that Mary conceived the Lord through her ear seem to have originated with Augustine—as has been shown by J. H. Waszink, art. 'Empfängnis' in *RAC* IV, 1253, against P. Langlois, art. 'Dracontius', *ibid.*, col. 259.

Augustine's own original idea to think about the problem of Mary's sinlessness; it was Pelagius who, in his fight against the universality of sin, first threw it into the debate against Augustine, without suspecting how far it would go.

Pelagius in his work *On Nature* wrote out a list of biblical characters, beginning with Abel, for whom, in his opinion, sinfulness was excluded, and he ended the list with Jesus' mother. To this Augustine gave an answer whose scope and meaning have repeatedly been the subject of dispute since the twelfth century, and on which even today there is no complete agreement. Augustine rejects the Pelagian assertion as a whole, but in doing so he makes a reservation for the Virgin Mary, conceding her a special position from the point of view of possible sinlessness. The decisive sentence reads: 'Except the holy Virgin Mary, with regard to whom, if it is a question of sins, I would for the honour of the Lord (Christ) allow no discussion whatever—for how do we know how much greater was the measure of grace that was granted to her for the complete conquest of sins, when she was deemed worthy to conceive and bear him who undoubtedly had no sin at all?—except, therefore, this one virgin, all saintly men and women, if we could call them together and ask them whether they lived without sin whilst they were in this life, what can we suppose would be their answer? Would it be in the language of [Pelagius] or in the words of the Apostle John [I John 1.8]?'[1] Augustine therefore regards Mary as a special case, because it is no use trying to decide what degree of freedom from sin was necessary where Christ, the Saviour free from all sin, was to take on human flesh and be born. As Augustine emphasizes elsewhere, Christ alone was not 'conceived in sin', nor nourished in sins in his mother's womb; for his begetter was God, and she who conceived and bore him was a virgin. As we see, the line of thought has a strictly Christological orientation, and is not discussed and continued at all beyond what concerns Mary's person. Nor did Augustine ever

---

[1] *De natura et gratia* 36 (42) (Urba and Zycha, CSEL 60 [1913], 263f.): 'excepta itaque sancta uirgine Maria, de qua propter honorem domini nullam prorsus, cum de peccatis agitur, haberi uolo quaestionem—unde enim scimus, quid ei plus gratiae collatum fuerit ad uincendum omni ex parte peccatum, quae concipere ac parere meruit, quem constat nullum habuisse peccatum?— hac ergo uirgine excepta si omnes illos sanctos et sanctas, cum hic uiuerent, congregare possemus et interrogare, utrum essent sine peccato, quid fuisse responsum putamus, utrum hoc, quod iste dicit, an quod Joannes apostolus (I John 1.8)?'

return to this question afterwards. At first he had left open theoretically the possibility of a person's present sinlessness, although he would not assume it;[1] but in the course of the Pelagian dispute he consolidated his position in this matter and sharpened it further, and finally sinlessness is expressly excluded for all mankind.[2] Only Christ is completely pure, and now there is no longer anything said even about Mary. The one principle is repeated unwearyingly and always afresh, that all men are sinners and that they need Christ's redemption.[3] Accordingly it seems to me clear that the idea of Mary's personal sinlessness (original sin is not being considered in this connection)[4] is far from Augustine's thoughts, and that he has no theological interest in that particular problem as such. What alone remains basic for him, even in the passage in question, is the birth of Christ himself, which is unique and in every respect entirely without sin. Yet the decision' with regard to Mary may remain *in suspenso*—indeed, his first answer to Pelagius does not in any case go beyond this; the fact of the virgin birth has by now come to be regarded by him, too, from the point of view of preservation from original sin. That is the view that Augustine—with and without Ambrose's influence—expressly maintained in the conflict with the Pelagians and repeatedly substantiated,[5] and it determines the further development.

[1] *Perfect. iustit. homin.* 21.44; *Ep.* 157.2, 4.

[2] *C. duas epist. Pelag.* IV 10.27.

[3] Cf. the well-documented survey of the development in Friedrich, *Mariologie*, pp. 183–233.

[4] This, too, is, of course, disputed; but cf. besides Friedrich's presentation the 'critical marginal notes' by Fritz Hofmann, 'Die Stellung des heiligen Augustinus zur Lehre von der Unbefleckten Empfängnis Mariae', *TQ* 113 (1932), 299–319.

[5] It is hardly possible to quote all the relevant passages that Augustine, with or without relying on Ambrose (see p. 79, n 6.) takes into account or expressly develops. Sermons (as, e.g., *Serm.* 273.9 [Mai 95.7; in Morin, *S. Augustini sermones post Maurinos reperti*, p. 346]) and letters (such as *Ep.* 190 on infant baptism) are considered, too. The following passages may also be mentioned: *Peccat. merit. et remiss.* II 38; *Genes. ad litt.* X 20.35f.; *Nupt. et concupisc.* I 24.27: . . . 'in illo renascatur, quem sine ista concupiscentia uirgo concepit, propterea quando nasci est in carne dignatus, sine peccato solus est natus'; II 2.5; *C. duas epist. Pelag.* I 11.24; *C. Julian.* V 15.52; 54: 'quod autem attinet ad peccati originalis in omnes homines transitum, quoniam per concupiscentiam carnis transit, transire in eam carnem non potuit, quam non per illam uirgo concepit. [Christ's flesh] contagium uero peccati originalis non traxit, quia concumbentis concupiscentiam non inuenit'; *Corrept. et gratia* 11.30; *Opus imperf.* II 56; IV 5, 47f., 78f., 84, 87–89; VI 34f.

That means that in order that Christ should be born in absolute holiness, he did not obtain his human nature by means of sexual procreation; his conception and birth had to be immaculate. For the sexual act is not to be disconnected from sin—not indeed through the act as such, but through the inclination towards sensual appetite that undeniably clings to it;[1] and through it Adam's original lapse into a state of sin—which is broken through by Christ—is transmitted from generation to generation. Certainly, Mary's body, too, originated through carnal desire, but she could not pass it on into that body that was conceived without sensual appetite.[2] Thus, too, Christ would have no man as his father, because he would not come to men by the way of carnal desire.[3] Now Augustine found—more conclusively as time went on—the real abode of sin not by any means solely in the body and its sexuality, but above all in man's mind and will. It is from this point of view that, as a consequence of and punishment for the fall, man's nature has been perverted and corrupted into the realms of natural impulses. But as Augustine hesitates to put forward the idea of Adam's begetting a continuity of souls corresponding to a continuity of bodies,[4] he has no alternative but to put the transmission of original sin into the bodily sphere, and as the ascetic that he was and remained, he thus sees it directly

---

[1] We need not here enter into Augustine's laboured efforts, in view of the reproach of a 'Manichaean' bedevilment of nature and marriage, to follow out a distinction between the sin itself and the consequences or punishments of the sin in the domain of sex. J. Mausbach, *Die Ethik des heiligen Augustinus* 2 (1909), 173, rightly remarks that 'the ambiguity of certain linguistic expressions' (such as *malum*, *peccatum*, and occasionally even *concupiscentia*) 'creates a special source of misunderstandings'. But his own attempt to work out behind Augustine's pronouncements a basic point of view that is completely clear in itself implies, for that very reason, that Augustine was asking too much; and in effect it weakens his devaluation of the sexual. Cf., on the other hand, the presentation —perhaps a little one-sided in the opposite direction—given by E. Dinkler in *Die Anthropologie Augustins* (1934), 112ff., of the 'in itself somewhat confused doctrine of the *concupiscentia* as sexual pleasure and as sin', and J. Gross, *Entstehungsgeschichte des Erbsündendogmas. Von der Bibel bis Augustinus* (1960), 317–33, where it is regarded as incontestable that with Augustine 'the evaluation of sensual appetite as real sin predominates' (p. 328); further Jean Lebourlier, 'Misère morale originelle et responsabilité du pécheur', *Augustinus Magister* 3 (Paris 1955), 301–7.
[2] *Opus imperf.* V 62: 'Mariae corpus quamuis inde uenit, tamen eam non traiecit in corpus, quod inde non concepit'; cf. VI 22.
[3] *Sermo* 25 (Denis; Morin, p. 159): 'sed noluit hominem habere patrem, ne per concupiscentiam carnatam ueniret ad homines.'
[4] Cf. Dinkler, *Anthropologie*, pp. 121f.

bound up with the sexual nature of propagation. The consequences of this idea were momentous. For though Augustine's theory might carry little conviction to an opponent of Julian's calibre, it was bound to appeal to all the monks and celibate clergy who made up his following and were to provide all the ecclesiastical leaders of the future. Here, too, the semi-Pelagians raised no objection. Beside the practical ecclesiastical consistency of the indispensable baptism of infants, nothing contributed so quickly and universally to the recognition of Augustine's doctrine of original sin as its ascetic, anti-sexual motivation. 'Without carnal desire', as Fulgentius[1] paraphrases the Augustinian line of thought, 'there is no union of parents, and therefore the sons that are born of their flesh cannot be conceived without sin.'[2] On the other hand, 'Christ's flesh is indeed of the same nature as the flesh of all men, but the divine Word deigned to < take it and > unite it with himself from the Virgin Mary, and so it is nevertheless conceived without sin and born without sin.'[3] It is on this that salvation now depends.[4]

---

[1] On him see J. B. Bauer, 'De sancti Fulgentii Mariologia', *Marianum* 17 (1955), 531–5.

[2] *De fide* 16: 'sine libidine non est parentum concubitus. ob hoc filiorum ex eorum carne nascentium non potest sine peccato esse conceptus, ubi peccatum in paruulos non transmittit propagatio, sed libido. . . .'

[3] *De fide* 15: 'sed licet caro Christi et omnium hominum unius eiusdemque naturae sit, haec tamen quam deus verbum ex Maria virgine sibi unire dignatus est, sine peccato concepta, sine peccato nata est.'

[4] This is also shown, for example, in the theology of Leo the Great. In the *Tome*, partly formulated by Prosper (J. Gaidioz, 'Saint Prosper d'Aquitaine et le tome à Flavien', *Revue des Sciences religieuses* 23 [1949], 270–301), this point of view is only hinted at, Schwartz, *Acta conc. oecum.* II 2, p. 28: '. . . impassibilis deus non dedignatus est homo esse passibilis et immortalis mortis legibus subiacere; noua autem natiuitate generatus, quia inuiolata uirginitas concupiscentiam nesciuit, carnis materiam ministrauit.' The work is intended for the East. The idea appears the more forcibly in one of Leo's Christmas sermons, *Sermo* 22.3. Here we are told that the devil had obtained a certain legal claim on the human race, and that he had to be conquered if redemption were to become possible. Then the preacher goes on: 'quod ut fieret, sine uirili semine conceptus est Christus ex uirgine, quam non humanus coitus, sed spiritus sanctus fecundat. et cum in omnibus matribus non fiat sine peccati sorde conceptio, haec inde purgationem traxit, unde concepit. quo enim paterni seminis transfusio non peruenit, peccati se illic origo non miscuit. inuiolata uirginitas concupiscentiam nesciuit, substantiam ministrauit. assumpta est de matre domini natura, non culpa. creata est forma serui sine conditione seruili, quia nouus homo sic contemperatus est ueteri, ut et ueritatem susciperet generis et uitium excluderet uetustatis.' That is crude Augustinianism. Nor, as far as I can see, has Leo gone materially beyond Augustine elsewhere in his

Thus the originally separated themes of a Christological-theological and an Encratite-ascetic interpretation of the virgin birth have coalesced into a unity that remains. With that we have reached the end of the development in the early Church. The theory that brings it to a conclusion is, as we have seen, of western origin. In the East, where the ascetic concern in the *Apocryphon of James* and the testimony of Pseudo-Justin first found expression, it did not take root, for here there was no doctrine of original sin in the Augustinian sense. For Augustine himself the new western doctrine of the virgin birth had an exclusively Christological significance. But it nevertheless confirmed the older development of an ascetic glorification of Mary, and at the same time opened the way to a new expansion of 'Mariology'. The anti-Pelagian dogma remains a firm basis for the whole of the medieval and modern doctrine in the Roman Catholic Church, though, judged by their spirit, these later doctrines themselves and their ecclesiological and anthropological elements can no longer be regarded as having an Augustinian character or one typical of the early Church.

'Mariological' views. Alois Spindeler, 'Papst Leo I, über die Mitwirkung Marias bei der Erlösung', *Münchene theologische Zeitschrift* 10 (1959), 229–34, has similarly overinterpreted the Pope; and the same thing happens, though unjustly, to Augustine.

ADDITIONAL NOTE

I AVAIL myself of the opportunity afforded by the English edition to mention in this appended note a book which treats of the same subject as does this study. I regret that Dr Thomas Boslooper's book *The Virgin Birth* (London, 1962) did not come to my notice till after my book was completed. Here the field covered is substantially wider; the work treats of the entire history of the interpretation of the virgin birth and seeks in an ecumenical spirit to bring to light the significance lying concealed in a 'mythical' form. In the first chapters the author discusses numerous passages from the writings of the ancient Church and devotes a long chapter to the problem, which I have not dealt with, of pagan 'parallels'. Less emphasis is given to exploring and distinguishing the different lines of theological development within the ancient Church. I must not embark on a full discussion here, but merely mention this book, which develops as a theological problem the subject which I have treated from the point of view of the history of dogma.

INDEX OF ANCIENT AUTHORS

INDEX OF MODERN AUTHORS